A Teacher's Planning Guide to Fun Projects for Kids
Classroom Art Projects from September through May

VII. **MARCH:** Lions and Lambs; Wind; Kites; Moon Week; St. Patrick's Day

VIII. **APRIL:** Easter, Passover; Showers and Flowers; Animals

Library of Congress Cataloging in Publication Data

Neal, Judith F.
  Fun projects for kids.

  Summary: Presents projects for kindergarten and primary
school children to make with inexpensive household items as
part of a year-long art course in school or as quiet time
activity at home.
  1. Handicraft—Juvenile literature. [1. Handicraft]
I. Bellew, Mike, ill. II. Title.
TT160.N4 1983   745.5   83-7657
ISBN 0-516-00821-8

FUN PROJECTS for KIDS

Judith F. Neal

Illustrations by Mike Bellew

Delair Publishing Company, Inc.

Dedicated to:
Mother...teacher and artist

Acknowledgments

My grateful thanks to the teachers and staff of Lincolnwood
Preschool and Kindergarten whose advice, help and project
ideas have made this book possible, to Anna, without whom
the book could not have been written, and to Carl, whose patience and understanding made the work a joyful experience.

Delair Publishing Company, Inc.
420 Lexington Avenue
New York, New York 10170

Manufactured in the United States of America and published
simultaneously in Canada.

ISBN: 08326-2621-X

About this book . . .

Fun Projects for Kids is a happy trip into the wonderful world of art for kindergarten and primary school children. It can be used at home or in school. It can be used as a well-planned art course (which fits perfectly into the school year) or as quiet time activity at home.

The projects are designed to use common household items that are easily collected and inexpensive. Some projects do need special preparation or require time for collecting the materials. These projects are marked with a ✳ .

Each project will take about fifteen to thirty minutes.

Popsicle Stick Name Tags

☆ **Tools:**
glue
masking tape
crayons or markers

 ★ **Materials:**
popsicle stick
alphabet noodles

Directions

1. Color popsicle stick with bright color.
2. Apply layer of glue across stick and arrange noodles to spell name or message.
3. Double over masking tape and stick to back of popsicle stick to hold name tag onto shirt.

Me (A Shapes Person)

☆ **Tools:**
scissors
glue

★ **Materials:**
colored construction paper scraps
one sheet backing paper

Directions

1. Cut (or have pre-cut for younger children) circles, triangles, squares and rectangles from paper scraps.
2. Arrange on backing sheet to form the shape of a person.

This can be a simple project made with only six shapes or a more complicated figure, but use only the four basic shapes.

My House

☆ **Tools:**
scissors
glue
crayons

★ **Materials:**
colored construction paper pieces
one sheet backing paper

Directions

1. Cut (or have pre-cut for younger children) shapes from paper pieces.
2. Glue to backing sheet to make a picture of a house with rectangle door, square windows, etc.
3. Decorate with crayons.

My Family Tree

☆ **Tools:**
scissors
glue
crayons

★ **Materials:**
green and brown construction paper
one sheet backing paper

Directions

1. Cut one green circle for each family member, and a brown rectangle for the tree trunk.
2. Glue paper shapes to backing sheet.
3. Draw the face of each family member in the green circles.

Grandparents' Day Cards

☆ **Tools:**
scissors
glue
crayons or markers

★ **Materials:**
colored construction paper
magazine

Directions

1. Fold construction paper in half to make the card.
2. Cut pictures from magazines of things that grandparents use or enjoy—or things that remind us of our grandparents.
3. Glue collage of pictures on the front of the card, and a message can be written inside.

Leaf Collection

☆ **Tools:**
glue
iron for pressing waxed paper

★ **Materials:**
leaves collected from nature walk
one sheet construction paper for frame
two large sheets of waxed paper

Directions

1. Arrange leaves on top of one sheet of waxed paper.
2. Cover with second sheet of waxed paper and press with hot iron to fuse the waxed paper sheets together.
3. Cut out the center of the construction paper to make a frame for the leaves, and glue to waxed paper.

Note: Save some of the leaves for project on Wednesday. If the leaves are put between sheets of newspaper and left under a weight overnight, they will be pressed flat and easier to work with.

Sponge Paint Leaf Shape

☆ **Tools:**
pieces of torn sponge
scissors

★ **Materials:**
one sheet orange construction paper
tempera paint in fall colors (red, green, brown, yellow)
flat containers such as aluminum pans to hold paint

Directions

1. Cut a large oval shape from the orange construction paper (jagged edges, stem at one end) to make the leaf shape.
2. Sponge paint onto shape, overlapping colors.

(This leaf shape could also be covered with small squares of crumpled tissue in fall colors using glue to hold the tissue.)

Leaf Person

☆ **Tools:**
glue
crayons

★ **Materials:**
leaves collected from nature walk
one sheet construction paper

Directions

1. Glue a large leaf to the center of the sheet of construction paper—this is the "body" of the leaf person.
2. With crayons, draw arms, legs and head onto the body. Other small leaves can be glued onto the paper for extra decoration, such as a "hat", "shoes" or "skirt".

Fill-In Shapes

☆ **Tools:**
glue
crayons or markers

✱ ★ **Materials:**
popcorn (popped)
birdseed
one sheet construction paper

Directions

1. Draw (or have pre-drawn for younger children) the four basic shapes: square, triangle, circle and rectangle.
2. Cover each shape individually with glue.
3. Sprinkle birdseed over two shapes; cover two shapes with popcorn.

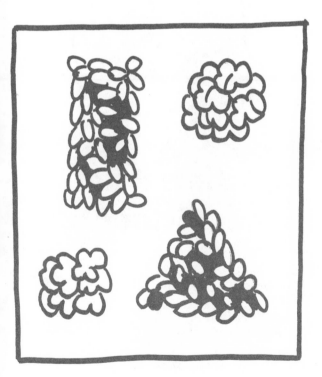

Fall Colors Collage

☆ **Tools:**
scissors
glue
pencil

★ **Materials:**
paper scraps in fall colors
one sheet construction paper

Directions

1. Draw the four basic shapes on colored construction paper scraps.
2. Cut out with scissors and glue to contruction paper backing sheet.
3. Several shapes in each color should be used.

Soap Paint Picture

☆ **Tools:**
paint brush

★ **Materials:**
*soap paint using brown tempera
(see page 124)
paint tray
one sheet construction paper*

Directions

1. Paint a picture using the brown soap paint.
2. You may suggest a fall theme—a squirrel, a tree with falling leaves, a bear—or let the child paint his own creation.
3. The heavy texture of the paint and the monocolor painting is important here, not artistic ability!

Blow Paint Picture

 ☆ **Tools:**
plastic or paper straw

★ **Materials:**
*liquid tempera paint
teaspoon
one sheet construction paper*

Directions

1. Drop a teaspoon of paint onto the middle of the construction paper.
2. Blow through the straw (gently!) to spread the paint around the paper.

Marble Painting

☆ **Tools:**

shoe box lid or any similar container
marble, ball bearing or small rubber ball

★ **Materials:**

liquid tempera paint
teaspoon
manila paper cut to fit inside box lid or similar container

Directions

1. Place the manila paper inside the box lid.
2. Drop a teaspoon of paint onto the paper.
3. The child rolls the marble back and forth through the paint to make designs on the paper.
4. Using two colors of paint make an even more dramatic effect—especially when they blend to make a third color.

Shapes Mobile

☆ **Tools:**

scissors
glue
tape
pencil

★ **Materials:**

large construction paper scraps
piece of yarn 2-3 feet in length

Directions

1. Draw the four basic shapes, each in a different color, and cut from construction paper.
2. Draw them again, this time slightly smaller, and in different colors of paper.
3. Cut out these shapes and glue one in the center of each of the larger shapes.
4. Line up the four large pieces, lay the piece of yarn across them and secure with tape.

Blot Painting

☆ **Tools:**
teaspoon
crayons or markers

★ **Materials:**
liquid paint
one sheet manila paper

Directions

1. Drop a teaspoon of paint in the center of the manila sheet.
2. Fold the paper in half and rub to disperse the paint.
3. Unfold.
4. Outline the design with crayon or marker.
5. Talk about what the child's picture looks like to him—use crayons to decorate this "accidental picture."

Trace Foot

☆ **Tools:**
pencil
crayons
paint brush

★ **Materials:**
thin, liquid tempera paint wash
paint container
one sheet construction paper

Directions

1. Trace foot on construction paper using the pencil.
2. Color inside the foot shape with crayons.
3. Using the thin tempera paint, brush paint over entire sheet of paper—the paint will not stick to the crayon on the foot shape.

Me
(Paper Plate Face)

☆ **Tools:**
scissors
glue
crayons

★ **Materials:**
one small paper plate for each
  child
selection of yarn in several colors: black, yellow, red, brown

Directions

1. Each child chooses yarn the color of his own hair.
2. With scissors, cut the yarn into the desired length and glue to paper plate.
3. Color in face with emphasis on using the right color for the child's own eyes, skin, etc.

Vegetable Printing

☆ **Tools:**
available vegetables cut in half,
  such as: green peppers,
  mushrooms, brussel sprouts,
  potatoes (carve out pieces
  from the flat side so potatoes
  will print an interesting
  design.)

★ **Materials:**
liquid tempera paint
paint tray
one sheet construction paper

Directions

1. Dip vegetable into paint.
2. Gently shake off excess paint.
3. Press firmly onto construction paper.

Falling Acorns

Crayon On Sandpaper

☆ **Tools:**
glue
brown crayon

★ **Materials:**
1" green tissue squares
6 or 7 small cotton puffs
powdered brown tempera paint
paint tray
one sheet construction paper

☆ **Tools:**
crayons
iron

 ★ **Materials:**
one sheet construction paper
one sheet fine grain sandpaper
  (for each child).

Directions

1. Pressing firmly, color a picture onto the sandpaper.
2. Lay the sandpaper over the sheet of construction paper and press with hot iron for about ten seconds.
3. The crayon will melt and the picture will be transferred onto the paper.

Directions

1. Draw two vertical lines in the middle of the sheet of construction paper (this is the tree trunk.)
2. Glue green tissue squares to the top of the tree trunk to form the leaves.
3. Roll cotton puffs in powdered paint.
4. Apply glue to the bottom of the picture and glue brown cotton puff "acorns" under the tree.

"My Favorite Things"

☆ **Tools:**
crayons or markers

★ **Materials:**
*one sheet manila or construction
paper*

Directions

1. Draw two lines and divide the paper into four equal parts.
2. Label each of the four sections according to the child's interest and draw a picture to illustrate.
3. Examples: My Favorite Pet, My Favorite Superhero, My Favorite Food, My Favorite Person, My Favorite Toy, My Favorite Activity, My Favorite Season.

Spatter or Sponge Paint

☆ **Tools:**
*toothbrush (for spatter painting)
or sponges (for sponge paint)
glue*

★ **Materials:**
*leaves
one sheet manila or construction
   paper
liquid tempera paint
paint tray
(a large cardboard box should be
   available if the spatter project
   is selected)*

Directions

SPATTER PAINTING

1. With a drop of glue, secure a large leaf to the center of the manila paper.
2. Place the paper into a cardboard box (to prevent paint spattering in the wrong places).
3. Dip the toothbrush into the tempera paint and let the child rub his thumb over the bristles to flick the paint onto the paper.
4. When the picture is dry, remove the leaf.

SPONGE PAINTING

1. Glue the leaf to the paper as explained above.
2. Dip the sponge piece into the paint.
3. Sponge paint around the leaf.
4. When dry, remove the leaf.

Shapes Clown

☆**Tools:**
scissors
glue

★**Materials:**
*construction paper scraps in
    several colors*
*one sheet construction paper for
    backing*

Directions

1. Cut a large circle for the face, a large triangle for the hat, and a large rectangle for the collar.
2. Cut colored circles for the eyes and nose; cut squares for the ears. (Younger children may need to have these shapes pre-drawn for them).
3. Glue the shapes to the backing sheet to form a clown. (Any available trim, such as stick-on colored stars would be fun to use with this project.)

Universal Children's Day Picture

☆**Tools:**
scissors
glue
crayons

★**Materials:**
one sheet manila paper
one sheet construction paper

Directions

1. To cut paper dolls, fold short edge of paper over about 1½ inches then fold back the opposite direction about 1½ inches.
2. Continue the back and forth folding as if making a fan.
3. Hold the folded paper with the first open edge toward the scissors and cut out one half of a figure.
4. Do not cut across arm so that, when unfolded, the three figures will be joined at the hand. (Even the crudest attempt at cutting a figure will show rewarding result when the paper is unfolded.)
5. Glue the figures to the sheet of construction paper, and decorate with crayons.

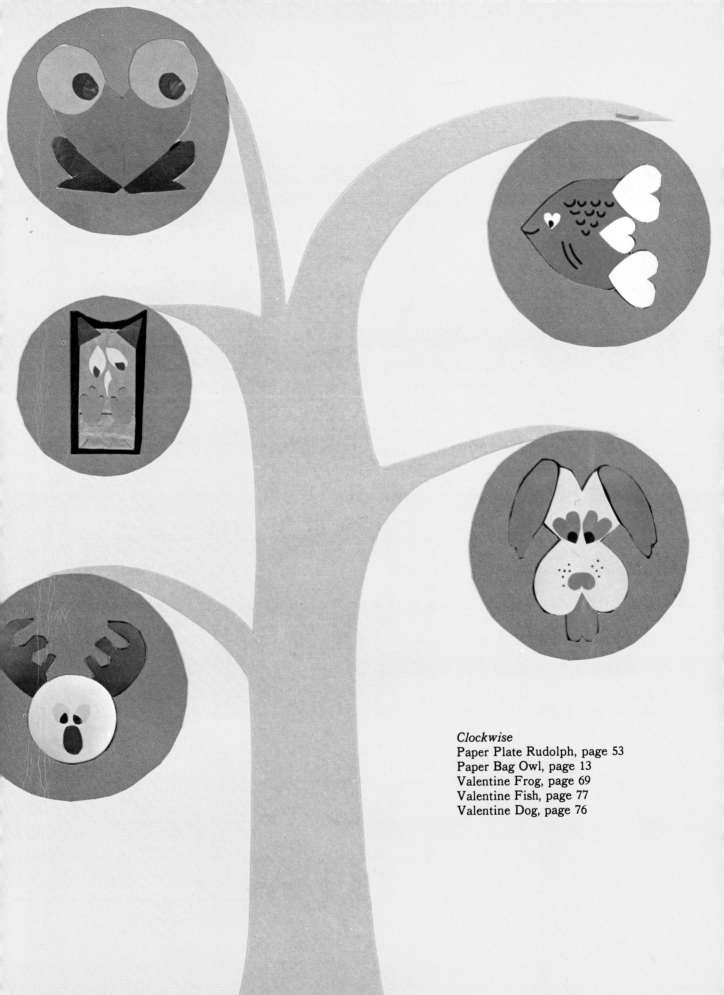

Paper Bag Owl

☆ **Tools:**
scissors
glue

★ **Materials:**
orange, brown, white and yellow construction paper scraps
small brown paper bag

Directions

1. Cut two brown triangles (ears), two large white and two small brown circles (eyes), two large orange triangles—or any shape—(feet), and a small yellow triangle (beak) from construction paper scraps.
2. Glue feet to bottom flap of bag, ears to top, open edge of bag, and eyes and beak to the side of the bag.
3. Show the children how the placement of the small brown circle inside the large white circle can make the owl show different expressions on his face.

Birdfeeder (1 and 2)

☆ **Tools:**
hole puncher

★ **Materials:**
Type 1: toilet tissue cardboard roll
Type 2: pine cone
Both: peanut butter
    birdseed
    short piece of yarn for hanging feeder
    plate
    small piece of newspaper

Directions

1. If using toilet tissue roll, punch holes near one end and string yarn through so that it can be hung in a tree.
2. If using pine cone, tie yarn around one end.
3. Sprinkle birdseed in the plate.
4. Smear either pine cone or tissue roll with peanut butter, and roll in birdseed.
5. Wrap the birdfeeder in the newspaper unless it is to be hung outside right away.

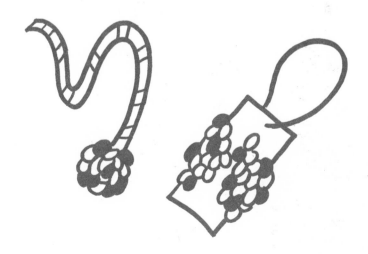

Bear Cub

☆ **Tools:**
scissors
glue

✱ ★ **Materials:**
scraps of material, fur,
wallpaper samples—anything
with texture—in dark brown,
black or grey color
one sheet construction paper if
free-form drawing, or prepared
ditto if this method is preferred

Directions

1. If preparing ditto, stencil or other method of mass copying, select and trace a picture of a bear as you would with other classroom activity stencils.
2. The artistic quality is not important here—the bear cub can be an oval with ears.
3. The object of this exercise is to layer the materials over the bear figure to create a three dimensional, textured picture, using glue to hold the fabric pieces in place. (The bear was chosen because it is an animal that changes its environment and way of life in the fall. A squirrel or rabbit or a turtle could just as easily be used.)

Squirrel Finger Puppet

☆ **Tools:**
scissors
glue
crayons or markers

✱ ★ **Materials:**
empty peanut shells
one sheet brown construction
paper

Directions

1. To draw a squirrel: Large circle body, small circle head, two triangles for ears, large oval shape for tail.
2. With scissors, cut out the figure and fringe the oval tail.
3. Cut two small finger holes near the top of the large circle body.
4. Features can be crayoned in using the basic shapes: circles for eyes, triangle nose, two small rectangles for teeth.
5. Glue empty peanut shells near bottom of the large circle body.

Columbus Day Boat

☆ **Tools:**
scissors
glue

★ **Materials:**
2 popsicle sticks
white and black construction
  paper scraps
1 sheet blue construction
  paper for backing

Directions

1. Using black and white paper scraps, cut two small white triangles (flags), two medium sized white triangles (sails) and one large black triangle (body of the boat).
2. Cut one corner off the large black triangle and discard.
3. Glue the black piece to the bottom of the blue page so that the longest edge is facing up.
4. Glue the popsicle sticks (masts) to the top edge of the boat, one at each end.
5. Glue the sails to the masts, making sure they are both facing the same way.
6. Glue the small white flags to the top of the masts.

Buffalo Halloween Mask

☆ **Tools:**
scissors
glue
glue brush

★ **Materials:**
brown tissue paper
*1 sheet black construction
    paper*
*short lengths of brown
    yarn—about 20 pieces cut 4"
    long*
1 large potato chip box
gold glitter

Directions

1. Cut strips of brown tissue paper about 4" wide and 24" long.
2. You will need five or six of these to cover the box.
3. Fringe the edges of the strips.
4. Cut the flaps off one end of the box and turn it upside down so that the open end is at the bottom.
5. Start at the bottom and work up—apply glue, then wrap one of the fringed tissue pieces around the box.
6. Apply another layer of glue around the top edge of the tissue, and glue on another fringed piece so that the fringe falls down over the first piece.
7. Continue in this manner until the box is covered with fringed tissue.
8. Cut small squares or pieces of tissue and glue across top (sealed flaps) of the box.
9. Make sure enough tissue is used to completely cover the potato chip box.
10. Dot the front of the box with glue, make loops with the short yarn pieces and press the cut ends onto the glue dots.
11. This will make the buffalo's face appear very shaggy.
12. Cut horns, eyes and nose from the sheet of black construction paper, and glue to front of box.
13. Dot glue on black paper eyes and sprinkle with glitter.
14. Extra pieces of brown yarn can be glued on top.
15. Once the potato chip box has been covered with any color tissue, this basic Halloween mask idea can be made to look like any animal or monster that time, materials available and the child's creativity will allow.

Haunted House

☆ **Tools:**
scissors
glue
crayons

★ **Materials:**
orange and yellow construction
   paper scraps
1 sheet white construction
   paper
1 sheet black construction
   paper

Directions

1. With black construction paper, cut a square house with a triangle roof.
2. Cut a large door in the square shape and fold it open.
3. Glue the house shape to the white construction paper.
4. Cut a moon shape from the yellow paper; cut an orange pumpkin shape from the orange paper.
5. Glue the moon above the house, and the pumpkin on the ground near the door.
6. With crayons, draw a ghost, skeleton, witch or scary figure inside the open door.
7. Decorate the picture with crayons: stars can be drawn in the sky, trees and grass around the house, etc.
8. Optional trims: Glue-on gold and silver stars, black yarn "smoke" coming from a chimney, crumpled white tissue ghost, gold glitter eyes and mouth on the pumpkin.

Pumpkin Plate Mask

Paper Plate Witch

☆ **Tools:**
scissors
glue
pencil

✱ ★ **Materials:**
1 sheet orange construction
   paper
black construction paper scraps
1 large paper plate
1 popsicle stick

Directions

1. Trace circle around the paper plate on the piece of orange paper.
2. Cut out with scissors and glue to paper plate.
3. Cut three triangles and funny mouth from black paper scraps.
4. Glue to orange plate circle.
5. Glue popsicle stick to back of plate.

☆ **Tools:**
scissors
glue

✱ ★ **Materials:**
1 small paper plate
red, orange and black construction paper scraps
corn husks for hair (yarn may be
   used if corn husks are difficult
   to obtain)
Indian corn kernels, popcorn or
   small nut shells for teeth

Directions

1. Cut large red oval mouth, two orange triangle eyes, one small black triangle nose and one large black triangle for witch's hat.
2. Glue to paper plate.
3. Glue corn husks on sides of plate for hair.
4. Glue corn kernels or shells over red oval for teeth.

Lighted Pumpkin

☆ **Tools:**
scissors
glue
black crayon or marker

★ **Materials:**
1 sheet orange construction
  paper
small green construction paper
  scrap
yellow tissue paper (or yellow or
  orange cellophane if available)

Directions

1. Draw a large circle on the orange paper and cut out with scissors.

2. Draw triangle eyes and funny mouth on the orange circle and cut out.

3. Cut green cap with jagged edge and glue to top of pumpkin.

4. Cut yellow tissue paper into pieces large enough to fit over the eye and mouth holes and glue them over the holes on the back of the pumpkin.

5. Use crayon to outline eyes and mouth, write a message or further decorate the pumpkin face.

6. When held up to the light, or taped to a window, the light will shine through the tissue over the eyes and mouth, and the pumpkin will appear to be lighted.

Pop-Up Ghost

☆ **Tools:**
scissors
glue or tape
black marker

★ **Materials:**
1/4 sheet white construction
  paper
popsicle stick
styrofoam cup

Directions

1. Using marker, draw a ghost or scary shape on the white paper.

2. Cut out this shape with scissors.

3. Glue popsicle stick to back of ghost.

4. Use the end of the popsicle stick to punch a hole in the bottom of the cup.

5. Insert the ghost into the cup, stick first, and make the ghost pop out of the cup by pushing up the stick.

Scary Picture

☆ **Tools:**
white chalk

★ **Materials:**
*1 sheet black construction
  paper
spray starch*

Directions

1. Draw ghosts, skeletons, tombstones, witches, jack o'lantern, a cloudy moon and other Halloween figures.
2. Spray with starch to fix the chalk.

Paper Bag Ghost

☆ **Tools:**
*scissors
glue
paint brush*

★ **Materials:**
*1 small brown paper bag
small black construction paper
  scrap
white tempera paint
paint container*

Directions

1. Cut two small circles from black paper for the ghost's eyes.
2. Open bag, turn upside down (open end down) and paint with white paint.
3. Glue black circle eyes to front of bag.
4. When dry, this bag can be used for small, party treat bag.

"Trick or Treat" Bag

Black Cat Finger Puppet

☆ **Tools:**
scissors
glue
white chalk

★ **Materials:**
1 sheet black construction
  paper
gold glitter

Directions

1. With white chalk, draw shape cat on black paper: large circle body, small circle head, triangle ears.
2. Cut out cat shape with scissors.
3. Near bottom of large circle body, cut two small finger holes.
4. Use chalk to draw eyes, nose, mouth and whiskers.
5. Over drop of glue on each eye, sprinkle gold glitter.

☆ **Tools:**
scissors
glue
crayons

★ **Materials:**
1 large brown grocery bag
1 sheet white construction
  paper
1 sheet orange construction
  paper
1 sheet black construction
  paper

Directions

1. With yellow crayon, draw cat shape on black construction paper. (See *Black Cat Finger Puppet,* this page).
2. Draw ghost on white paper, and pumpkin on orange paper.
3. Cut the figures out with scissors, and glue pieces to paper bag.
4. Handles can be made by gluing strips cut from scraps across top of bag.
5. Use crayons to decorate and personalize treat bag.

UN Day Flag (October 24)

☆ **Tools:**
crayons

★ **Materials:**
prepared ditto (if this method is preferred) or one sheet white construction paper

Directions

1. Color picture of United States flag with crayons.
2. If teaching children to draw the flag: draw a large rectangle with a small square in the upper left corner.
3. Draw eleven horizontal lines across the rectangle.
4. Color alternate stripes, beginning with red.
5. Stars or small representative circles should be drawn inside the square and colored yellow.
6. Fill in the square with blue crayon.

Jack O'Lantern

☆ **Tools:**
scissors
glue

★ **Materials:**
2 sheets orange construction paper
1 sheet black construction paper

Directions

1. Fold one sheet orange paper in half, lengthwise.

2. Starting at folded edge, make cuts one inch apart to within one inch of outside edge of paper.

3. Unfold paper and glue edges of cut paper together, top to bottom. (This is the lantern.)

4. Cut a circle from the other sheet of orange paper.

5. Cut two triangle eyes and funny mouth shape from sheet of black paper.

6. Glue eyes and mouth to pumpkin face circle shape.

7. Cut two one-inch strips from long edge of black construction paper.

8. Fold one strip in half and glue pumpkin face to folded edge.

9. Drop this down inside the lantern and glue top of each side of the black strip to the top edges of the lantern.

10. Using the other black strip as the lantern's handle, glue ends of strip to top of lantern.

11. When the Jack O'Lantern is held by the handle, it appears to be a solid orange tube.

12. When set down, the cuts separate and the pumpkin shape within is revealed.

Bat and Spider

☆ **Tools:**
scissors
glue
tape
white chalk

★ **Materials:**
2 sheets black construction
  paper
4-5" length of yarn
gold glitter

Directions

BAT

1. Fold one sheet of black paper in half, top to bottom.
2. Work with folded edge to the left.
3. Using chalk, at top of paper, start at folded edge and make a large "W" which extends to the open edges of the paper.
4. At the bottom of the paper, start at folded edge and make a large "M" which extends to the open edges of the paper.
5. Using scissors, cut on chalk line.
6. Do not cut on folded edge of paper.
7. Round off open edges of paper to encourage bat shape.
8. Unfold.
9. Tape yarn to center of bat's back.

SPIDER

1. Fold second sheet of black paper in half and cut along fold line with scissors.
2. Draw hourglass shape on half sheet with chalk, and cut with scissors.
3. Fold other half sheet back and forth as in making a fan.
4. With scissors, cut across folded paper five times to make six legs.
5. Glue or tape legs to hourglass shape, three on each side.
6. Tape yarn to center of spider's

Harvest Foods

Plaster of Paris Pumpkins

☆ **Tools:**
bowl
spoon
paint brush or markers

✱ ★ **Materials:**
small box of plaster of Paris
1 large sheet of aluminum foil
water
orange, black and green tempera
  paint if markers are not used

Directions

1. Mix plaster of Paris according to package directions.
2. Drop by tablespoonsful onto aluminum foil sheet.
3. The plaster will dry quickly—within a half hour—and the circles can be colored with markers or painted with tempera paint.
4. These tiny plaster pumpkins make wonderful Halloween souveniers and can be decorated with green felt or paper stems, glitter, or other available trims.

✱ ★ **Materials:**
selection of available or unusual
  cooked or raw foods
chart drawn on large sheet of
  construction paper showing
  pictures of foods to be tasted
  and categories to be checked
paper napkins

Directions

1. To show the children that things are not always what they appear to be, and that tasting and exploring new foods can be fun, ask them to comment on what they expect the foods to taste like and write this down on your chart.
2. After they've tasted the foods, ask them for comments again.
3. Design the chart to fit your own specific needs.
4. Some examples of foods that are easy to prepare and that will stimulate the children's curiosity are: olives; green pepper strips; few kernels of fresh, uncooked corn; bites of avocado or cooked sweet potato; raw snow peas.

Magic Crayon Picture

☆ **Tools:**

crayons
pencil

★ **Materials:**

*1 sheet white construction
  paper*

Directions

1. Fold sheet of construction paper in half.
2. Unfold.
3. On one side color heavily with crayons—two or three dark colors—until the entire half page is covered with a thick layer of crayon.
4. Refold paper.
5. Draw a Halloween picture with the pencil, pressing firmly.
6. When the paper is opened the crayon will be transferred onto the half sheet opposite the crayoned side of the paper.

Carve a Pumpkin

☆ **Tools:**

knife
large spoon
*portable toaster oven, electric
  frypan or other means of
  roasting seeds, if this is to be
  done*
paint brush

★ **Materials:**

1 large pumpkin
vegetable oil
salt
black tempera paint

Directions

1. Adult carves the pumpkin and removes seeds.
2. Rinse seeds and roast in salt and vegetable oil.
3. On a cookie sheet, in a 350⁰ oven, the seeds will be toasted and ready to eat in about five minutes.
4. The process takes less time in a toaster oven or in an electric frypan.
5. The children will enjoy painting the pumpkin with the black paint while the seeds are toasting.
6. This is a good way to introduce the children to a new food, as well as enjoying a favorite class activity.

Scarecrow

☆ **Tools:**
scissors
glue
crayons or markers

✴ ★ **Materials:**
1 sheet construction paper
fabric scraps
construction paper scraps
2 popsicle sticks

Directions

1. Cut shirt, hat, pants and any extra trims from fabric scraps.
2. Cut small circle for scarecrow's face.
3. Cross popsicle sticks and glue to construction paper.
4. Over popsicle stick frame, glue fabric pieces and construction paper face.
5. Fray yellow or brown fabric to use for straw and hair, and glue to scarecrow.
6. Draw features on the face.

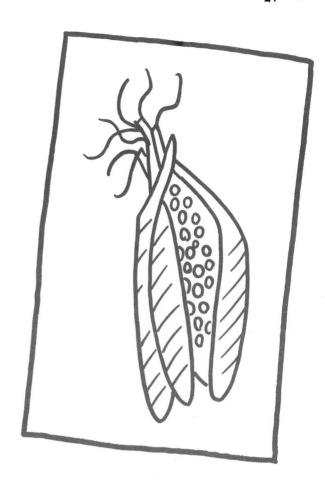

Corn Picture

☆ **Tools:**
glue
crayons or markers

✴ ★ **Materials:**
1 sheet construction paper
popcorn (unpopped)
corn husks
brown ribbon
fabric or paper scraps

Directions

1. Draw elongated oval shape on construction paper to make shape of an ear of corn.
2. Glue popcorn inside the oval shape, and glue corn husks around the edge.
3. Fringe brown ribbon or paper scraps (these are the cornsilks) and glue to the corn shape.

Black Crow

☆ **Tools:**
scissors
white chalk

✸ ★ **Materials:**
1 sheet black construction
* paper*
clothespin

Directions
1. Fold paper in half, lengthwise.
2. With chalk, draw side view of crow (oval body with beak, triangle shaped wings), with body on the folded edge.
3. Cut out with scissors.
4. Unfold and bend wings away from body.
5. Place clothespin in the middle of the crow's body so it will stand by balancing on its beak.

Paper Bag Indian

☆ **Tools:**
paint brush
glue or tape

✸ ★ **Materials:**
watercolors
container of water
small brown bag
small strip construction paper,
* 2" x 8"*
paper scraps
newspaper
rubber band

Directions
1. Stuff bag with newspaper and secure with rubber band.
2. Glue or tape 8" strip of construction paper around Indian's head.
3. Cut feathers from paper scraps and glue to headband.
4. Paint face with water colors.

Coffee Can Tom-Tom

☆ **Tools:**
paintbrush
glue

⭐ ★ **Materials:**
coffee can with plastic lid (or
oatmeal container, cut in half)
strip of construction paper cut to
fit around can or oatmeal con-
tainer
watercolors
container of water

Directions

1. Glue paper strip around coffee can (or oatmeal container).
2. With watercolors, decorate drum with Indian designs.
3. Do not paint plastic lid.
Children enjoy saving Indian and Pilgrim accessories to wear during Thanksgiving "feast" (last week of November).

Paper Bag Indian Vest

☆ **Tools:**
scissors
crayons

⭐ ★ **Materials:**
large brown grocery bag

Directions

1. Turn bag upside down and flatten.
2. Cut slit up the front, widening into "V" shape at neckline.
3. Continue cutting until a hole is made for the neck.
4. Cut two holes in sides of bag for arms.
5. Cut fringe at bottom of vest.
6. Decorate with crayons.

Indian Feather Headband

☆ **Tools:**
scissors
glue
crayons or markers

★ **Materials:**
*several sheets construction
  paper in different colors*

Directions

1. Cut two 2" strips from long edge of sheet of construction paper.
2. Glue (or staple) ends together.
3. Cut feather shapes from colored paper; fringe edges with scissors.
4. Decorate headband and feathers with crayons.
5. Glue feathers to inside of headband.
6. When dry, fit headband around child's head and glue (or staple) ends together.

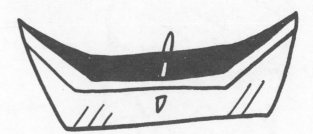

Indian Canoe

☆ **Tools:**
scissors
glue
paintbrush
pencil

★ **Materials:**
1/2 sheet construction paper
container of water
watercolors
toothpick

Directions

1. Fold construction paper in half, top to bottom.
2. With folded side as the bottom of the canoe, draw side view of Indian canoe and cut out with scissors.
3. Glue curved ends of canoe together.
4. Decorate with watercolors.
5. When glue is completely dry, separate sides of canoe and glue ends of toothpick to each side to keep canoe open.

Teepees; Peace Pipe

☆ **Tools:**
scissors
glue
paint brush

✶ ★ **Materials:**
*middle sections of cardboard egg
    carton*
toothpicks
watercolors
container of water
plastic straw
*brown construction paper rec-
    tangle cut 2" x 6"*
*construction paper scraps in dif-
    ferent colors*

Claydough Indian Pottery

Directions

1. Divide claydough into small por-tions.
2. Each small ball of claydough will make one bowl.
3. Poke a finger into a small ball and enlarge the hole to make the basic bowl shape.
4. Set aside to dry for one week.

Directions

TEEPEES

1. Cut triangular shaped doorway in each egg carton section.
2. Insert toothpicks in top.
3. Decorate teepees with watercolors.

PEACE PIPE

1. Fold brown paper rectangle over end of plastic straw and glue sides together.
2. Cut and fringe feathers from paper scraps.
3. Punch hole at bottom of each feather, and run straw through the holes.

Pilgrim Hat, Bonnet, Cuffs and Collar

☆ **Tools:**
scissors
glue
stapler
pencil

★ **Materials:**
1 large (12" x 18") sheet black
  construction paper
2 large sheets white construction
  paper
1 small size (12" x 9") sheet
  white construction paper
small strip yellow paper (9" x 3")
8 pieces yarn, 3-4" long

Directions

PILGRIM HAT
1. Cut 2" strip from long side of black paper. (Headband)
2. Measure 7" from top of remaining piece and cut. (Hat)
3. Measure 2" from top of remaining piece and cut. (Headband lengthener)
4. Measure 3" from top of remaining piece and cut. (Frontpiece)
5. Put the headband with the lengthener strip and staple (or glue) one end together.
6. Measure to fit child's head, and staple headband ends together.
7. Glue 7" strip inside headband.
8. Glue 3" strip to outside of headband in the middle of the strip only, so the ends stand apart from headband.
9. Fold yellow piece in half and cut "T" shape with square hole in top (top of "T" on the fold).
10. Glue this buckle to hat for trim.

COLLAR
1. Fold sheet of large white paper in half and cut off corners to make an oval shape.
2. Unfold and cut "V" shaped wedge in one side; continue cutting until a circle is made for the neck.
3. Punch holes at neckline.
4. Attach yarn ties.

CUFFS
1. Cut small sheet white paper in half.
2. Punch holes on two outside corners of each cuff.
3. Attach yarn ties.

BONNET
1. Fold back long edge of large sheet white construction paper to make a rim about 1" wide.
2. One the other long side of paper, cut in from both corners diagonally about 8".
3. Pull the outside angles together and staple at middle of the sheet of paper, forming a box-like shape.
4. With pencil, punch holes through folded edge near each end.
5. Attach yarn ties.

Coonskin Hat

☆ **Tools:**
scissors
glue
stapler
paint brush
pencil

★ **Materials:**
1 large (12" x 18") sheet brown
  construction paper
cotton puffs
brown tempera paint
paint tray

Directions

1. Cut a 3" strip from long side of brown paper. (Headband piece)
2. Cut a 3" strip across top of remaining piece. (Headband extender)
3. Attach headband to headband extender with glue or stapler.
4. Measure to fit child's head and glue headband ends together.
5. One edge of remaining piece of paper, trace a circle around the inside of headband.
6. Draw a second circle, about an inch larger, around the inside circle.
7. Cut around the outside circle line.
8. Cut tabs by cutting to inner circle line with small cuts about an inch apart. (These tabs will hold the top of the cap to the headband.)
9. Fold each tab in and apply a dot of glue to each tab, and glue top of cap to headband.
10. With remaining piece of brown paper, cut a large, oval-shape for the cap.
11. Gently separate cotton puffs, and glue to one side of the tail shape.
12. Paint three or four stripes across cotton with brown tempera paint.
13. Staple tail to edge of headband.

Paint
Indian Pottery

☆**Tools:**
paint brush

★**Materials:**
*claydough pottery made the
    week before*
brown and yellow tempera paint
paint trays
*(a can of spray shellac makes a
    very nice finish on the pottery,
    but this is not essential*

Directions
1. Paint pottery with Indian designs.
2. Finish with shellac if you wish.

Collage
Turkey Shape

☆**Tools:**
scissors
glue
crayons or markers

★**Materials:**
*1 sheet brown construction
    paper*
*orange, yellow and brown tissue
    paper squares*
*scrap piece red construction
    paper or felt*

Directions
1. Draw a simple turkey shape, or use this method: with fingers spread and thumb extended, trace around hand.
2. Thumb is turkey's neck and head—fingers are turkey's feathers—hand is turkey's body.
3. Cut out this shape.
4. Cut red wattle from scrap paper and glue onto turkey.
5. Crush tissue squares and glue onto tail area.
6. Draw eyes, wings with crayon.

Indian Sit-Upons; Thanksgiving Feast

☆ **Tools:**
scissors
crayons

★ **Materials:**
1 sheet brown construction paper
pan with an inch or so of water

Directions

1. Color Indian symbols and designs on brown construction paper.

2. Cut fringe around edges.

3. Crumple the paper into a ball, being careful not to tear it.

4. Smooth paper out with hands, and dip into water.

5. When dry, the "sit-upon" resembles the leather mats the Indians used.

Feast Idea

1. This is a good time to wear all the Indian and Pilgrim outfits you have made throughout the month.

2. Children enjoy having a pow-wow or feast with popcorn as you discuss the Thanksgiving theme and the contributions the first Americans made. (Or they can feast on corn muffins and homemade butter made by shaking whipping cream in cold jars until it solidifies).

Indian Village Scene

☆ **Tools:**
paint brush

★ **Materials:**
*1 sheet white construction
  paper*
watercolors
container of water

Directions

1. Paint an Indian scene: Teepees and canoes in a natural setting (trees, lake, mountains, sun, animals), Indians and their tools (bow and arrows, pottery), and their decorative costumes (feathers, fringed clothing and jewelry).

2. Creativity and individual expression should be stressed.

Indian Hand Shakers

☆ **Tools:**
glue
markers or crayons

★ **Materials:**
2 small paper plates
dried beans

Directions

1. Color Indian symbols on bottoms of plates.
2. Glue around outside edge.
3. Place a few beans inside one plate, and glue plates together.

Horn O'Plenty

☆ **Tools:**
scissors
glue

★ **Materials:**
old magazines
1 backing sheet construction
*   paper*
1 small sheet construction
*   paper*

Directions

1. Draw shape of cornucopia on brown paper.
2. Cut out the shape and glue to backing sheet.
3. Cut out pictures of foods from magazines and glue onto paper.

Wampum Necklace

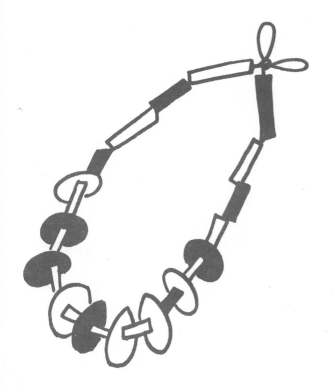

☆ **Tools:**
paintbrush

★ **Materials:**
mostaccioli or other uncooked
*   pasta with a hole through it*
yarn piece about 24" long
watercolors
container of water
small felt scrap circles with hole
*   punched in the middle*

Directions

1. Paint pasta.
2. When dry, string onto yarn.
3. Felt circles can be threaded between pasta pieces for an interesting design.

Walnut Turkey

Pilgrim Plate Mask

☆ **Tools:**
scissors
glue
markers

★ **Materials:**
walnut
feathers from a feather duster
  (if not available, cut feathers
  from brown tissue paper
small scrap of brown construc-
  tion paper

Directions
1. Draw a large "S" shape (about 2" high) on the brown paper scrap.
2. This is the turkey's head and neck. (Wattle and beak shape details can also be drawn, but not necessary.)
3. Cut out this shape, and glue to one end of the walnut shell by making a folded flap at the bottom of the paper.
4. Glue feathers to sides of the shell.
5. Use markers to color eyes, wattle and beak.

☆ **Tools:**
scissors
glue
crayons or markers

★ **Materials:**
large paper plate
1 sheet black construction
  paper
yellow paper scraps

Directions
1. Cut holes for eyes in paper plate.
2. Cut hat shape from black paper.
3. Cut buckle from yellow paper scraps.
4. Glue buckle onto hat.
5. Glue hat onto plate.
6. Color face with crayons.
(Rubber bands can be stapled on each side of the plate to stretch over the ears and hold the mask, but this is not necessary and sometimes difficult to do for an entire class).

Paper Plate Wreath

☆ **Tools:**
scissors
glue

★ **Materials:**
1 small paper plate
green and red tissue squares
red construction paper scrap

Directions

1. Cut a circle from the center of the paper plate and discard.

2. Apply glue to the plate wreath shape.

3. Crumple green tissue squares and cover the plate.

4. Dot with glue and use crumpled red tissue squares to decorate.

5. Cut a large bow from the red construction paper scrap and glue to the bottom of the wreath.

6. Optional trims: glitter, bits of aluminum foil or Christmas wrap paper.

Menorahs: Clay or Paper

☆ **Tools:**

For clay Menorah:
glue
paint brush
For paper Menorah:
glue
scissors
pencil

★ **Materials:**

For clay Menorah:
claydough (see page 124)
blue tempera
paint tray
birthday cake candle
For paper Menorah:
1 sheet blue construction paper
1 sheet white construction paper
9 yellow tissue squares (1"
 squares)
glitter

Directions

Clay Menorah
1. Roll small lump of clay into thick sausage shape.
2. Using candle, press into clay and make nine indentions to hold candles.
3. Form small amount of clay into a thick circle base shape, and carefully join the two clay pieces—a dot of glue will help keep the pieces secured.
4. When dry, the candle holder should be painted blue, and one candle may be glued in the center hole.

Paper Menorah
1. Using blue construction paper, draw Menorah as follows: triangle base, rectangle shape drawn horizontally across top corner of triangle, nine vertical rectangles to represent candles.
2. Cut out with scissors and glue to white construction paper.
3. Crumple tissue squares and glue one to top of each blue rectangle candle.
4. Dot with glue and glitter for candle flames.

Dreidel (Channuka Spinning Top)

☆ **Tools:**
scissors
tape
crayons

★ **Materials:**
*1 sheet blue construction
  paper*

Directions

1. To draw a dreidel: Fold blue paper in half, top to bottom.
2. Draw a large rectangle shape.
3. Under this rectangle draw a triangle shape with point down—(top edge of triangle and bottom edge of rectangle is the same line.)
4. Draw small square shape centered on the top of the rectangle.
5. Keeping paper folded, cut with scissors around outside lines of the dreidel shape so that both shapes are cut at once.
6. Draw a line dividing each shape in half, starting from center of the square and continuing to the bottom point of the triangle.
7. Using scissors, cut on this line from center of square to a point midway through one shape.
8. Cut on line from point of the triangle to a point midway through the other shape.
9. The two shapes can be joined by slipping one cut shape over the top of the other and taping to secure.
10. Use crayons to write numbers or decorate the dreidel.

Stuffed Ornament

☆ **Tools:**
scissors
glue
crayons or markers

★ **Materials:**
1 sheet manila paper
torn tissue or shredded
  newspaper for stuffing
small piece yarn or ribbon

Directions

1. Fold manila paper in half.
2. Draw a holiday symbol or picture.
3. Suggested ideas: bell, star, candy cane, stocking, Christmas tree, angel or other simple shape.
4. Color with crayons.
5. Keeping paper folded, cut out the shape so that both pieces are cut at once.
6. Layer torn tissue or newspaper between the two pieces.
7. Glue edges of manila paper together.
8. Loop yarn or ribbon, and glue to stuffed ornament.

Eggshell Tree Trim

☆ **Tools:**
glue
transparent tape

★ **Materials:**
1 half empty eggshell for each
  child
glitter
short piece of ribbon

Directions

1. Tape ribbon carefully to one side of the eggshell.
2. Cover inside of shell with glue and sprinkle with glitter.

Paper Gingerbread Man

☆ **Tools:**
scissors
glue
pencil

★ **Materials:**
1 sheet brown construction paper
Use available candy decorations—suggestions: raisin eyes, rice cereal sprinkled over hands and feet, cookie decorations or small hard candies for buttons, mouth and nose.

Directions

1. To draw a gingerbread man: Large circle body, small circle head, elongated ovals for arms and legs, small circles for feet and hands.
2. Cut out the shape with scissors.
3. Use glue and candy and cereal trims to decorate the gingerbread man.
4. This gingerbread man shape can also be traced around a large cookie cutter, if one is available.

Santa Paper Plate Mask

☆ **Tools:**
scissors
glue
crayons

★ **Materials:**
1 large paper plate
1 sheet red construction paper
cotton puffs

Directions

1. Cut two holes in the center of the paper plate for eyes.
2. Cut large red triangle hat from construction paper and glue to top of paper plate.
3. Glue cotton puffs along bottom edge of hat, and at top corner of triangle to decorate.
4. Glue cotton along bottom of plate for beard.
5. Draw Santa's nose and mouth, and color face with crayon.

Channuka Decoration

scissors
tape
pencil

★ **Materials:**
1 sheet blue construction
  paper
1 sheet white construction
  paper
4 short lengths of yarn

Directions

1. On sheet of blue paper, begin in the center of the page and draw continuous, ever-widening circles until pencil reaches the edge of the paper.
2. Cut with scissors on this line.
3. Tape a length of yarn to the center of the paper so that it may be hung from the ceiling.
4. On sheet of white paper, draw three triangles.
5. Over each triangle, draw another, inverted triangle—this will make the shape of the Star of David.
6. Cut these stars out with scissors, and tape a length of yarn to the top of each star.
7. Tape stars to shape cut from blue paper.

Angel

☆ **Tools:**
scissors
crayons

★ **Materials:**
1 sheet red construction paper
1 sheet yellow construction
  paper

Directions

1. Draw an angel: circle head, triangle body, rectangle arms.
2. Cut the angel shape from the yellow construction paper.
3. Color with crayons.
4. Draw angel wings on red paper: two large bell shapes joined at one edge to make a bow.
5. Cut wing shape out with scissors; round off edges.
6. Glue wings to back of angel.
7. Cut vertical slits on each side of wings and slip angel's arms through slits.
8. Optional trim: gold glitter on wings.

Christmas Tree

☆ **Tools:**
scissors
glue
tape
pencil

★ **Materials:**
*2 sheets green construction
  paper*
popcorn (popped) for tree trims

Directions

1. Draw a Christmas tree shape (simple shape—a large triangle), and with scissors cut both sheets of green paper at once.

2. Draw a line dividing each shape in half, from top corner of triangle to bottom base line.

3. With scissors, cut on this line from top corner of triangle to a point midway through the shape on one piece of green paper.

4. Cut from bottom base line, midway through shape on the other green paper.

5. The two shapes can be joined by slipping one cut shape over the top of the other and taping to secure.

6. The Christmas tree will stand alone.

7. Dot the tree with glue and decorate with popcorn trim.

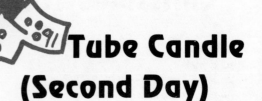

Tube Candle (First Day)

☆ **Tools:**
scissors
glue

 ★ **Materials:**
1 toilet tissue tube
3" circle cut from cardboard
red construction paper scraps
gold or green foil wrapping
  paper if available—otherwise
  use green construction paper
  scraps

Directions

1. Trace circle around piece of cardboard on red construction paper.
2. Cut out the red circle and make 1" cuts around edge of paper.
3. Bend flaps in.
4. Apply glue to one end of toilet tissue roll, and cover end of roll with red paper circle.
5. Glue around bottom edge of tube and stand tube up on the center of the cardboard base.
6. Leave to dry overnight.
7. Cut small red teardrop shape (or triangle) from scrap paper for candle flame.
8. Cut holly leaf shapes (or triangles) from foil wrapping paper or green construction paper.

This is a two-day project.

Tube Candle (Second Day)

☆ **Tools:**
glue
paint brush

★ **Materials:**
red tempera paint
paint tray
red and gold glitter
tissue wrapping paper

Directions

1. Paint toilet tissue tube, cardboard circle base and red paper covering end with red tempera paint.
2. While paint dries, decorate small triangle flame shape and foil (or green paper) holly leaf shapes with red and gold glitter sprinkled over glue designs.
3. Glue flame shape to top of candle.
4. Glue holly leaf shapes to candle's base.
5. Drizzle a little glue down the side of the candle and around the base, and sprinkle with gold glitter.
6. This holiday candle table decoration is ready to be wrapped in tissue and taken home for a special gift.

Holiday Card

☆ **Tools:**
scissors
glue
markers

★ **Materials:**
1 sheet blue construction
  paper
black paper scraps
small white tissue squares
glitter

Directions

1. Fold sheet of blue paper in half.
2. On front of card draw snowman using three circles for basic shape.
3. Cover circles with glue.
4. Crumple tissue and glue each piece to snowman shape.
5. Cut black hat shape and glue to top of snowman's head.
6. Use marker to make features and write holiday message.
7. Sprinkle glitter over glue dots for snowman's buttons.

Star Santa

☆ **Tools:**
scissors
glue
crayons or markers

★ **Materials:**
1 sheet yellow construction
  paper
scrap paper
cotton puffs
silver glitter

Directions

1. Draw a star in the center of the yellow paper. (To make a pattern, cut a triangle shape from the scrap paper. Use this piece to trace around corners for five pointed star.)
2. Cut out the star shape and color red hat at top point, red Santa suit, black points at bottom for boots.
3. Color a black belt across the middle of the star.
4. Draw Santa's eyes and nose with crayons.
5. Use glue and cotton puffs to make Santa's beard.
6. Glue cotton puff ball at top corner of hat.
7. Drop a dot of glue at corner of one eye and sprinkle with silver glitter. This is the twinkle in our Star Santa's eye!

Stained Glass Window

☆ **Tools:**
scissors
tape
crayons
paint brush

★ **Materials:**
1 sheet colored construction
   paper
1 sheet manila paper
vegetable oil
paint tray

Directions

1. On manila paper draw four or five criss-cross lines with the black crayon.
2. Color each of the resulting sections with a different color crayon.
3. "Paint" over entire page with vegetable oil.
4. When the oil is absorbed and dry (next day), the manila paper will appear translucent, and light shining through will give a stained glass window effect.
5. To make a frame, cut a large rectangle shape from the center of the construction paper.
6. Tape this frame to the crayoned manila paper.

Rocking Horse

☆ **Tools:**
scissors
glue

★ **Materials:**
1 sheet red construction paper
glitter

*SPECIAL PREPARATION NEEDED: Make rocking horse pattern and trace shape on each sheet of red paper used. To make pattern draw oval shape for body, small oval head, two short, rectangles for legs. Have horse standing on curved, half-moon (rocker) shape. Cut along outside line for rocking horse pattern. Fold each sheet of red paper in half, top to bottom. Place pattern so that top of horse is at folded edge. Trace.

Directions

1. Cut out rocking horse shape.
2. Do not cut on folded edge.
3. Decorate with crayons—draw horse's eyes, mouth, mane, legs and tail on red paper.
4. Decorate saddle and rocker edge with glitter.
5. This paper horse will stand alone when unfolded and does rock back and forth.

Egg Carton Bell

☆ **Tools:**
scissors
glue

★ **Materials:**
1 cardboard egg carton section
  for each bell
colored pipe cleaner
sequins, if available
glitter
1 small, metal jingle bell for
  each egg carton section (These
  are sold by the package and
  are inexpensive and easy to
  find around holiday time.)

Directions

1. Cut jagged edge around outside of egg carton cup.
2. Punch hole in top.
3. Thread pipe cleaner through the metal bell and pull through top of egg carton cup.
4. Decorate cardboard cup with sequins and glitter.

Lighted Tree

☆ **Tools:**
scissors
glue
pencil

★ **Materials:**
1 sheet green construction
  paper
small squares of colored tissue
  paper

Directions

1. Fold green paper in half, top to bottom.
2. Draw Christmas tree shape (simple shape: large triangle).
3. Draw four or five small circles inside the tree shape.
4. Keeping paper folded, cut out the circles.
5. Unfold paper and cover half sheet inside with glue.
6. Lay colored tissue over holes, then fold the green paper over the tissue so both pieces are glued together.
7. Cut out Christmas tree shape.
8. When held up to the light, or taped to a window, the tissue over the holes will allow light to shine through, and the tree ornaments will appear to glow.

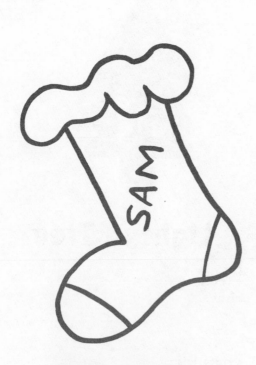

Red Paper Stocking

☆ **Tools:**
scissors
glue
pencil

★ **Materials:**
1 sheet red construction paper
cotton puffs
glitter

Directions

1. Draw a stocking shape on the red paper.
2. Cut the shape out with scissors.
3. Glue cotton puffs to top of stocking shape.
4. Names can be written on the stocking and decorated with glue and glitter.
5. This makes a nice bulletin board or holiday room decoration.

Sequined Decoration

☆ **Tools:**
cookie cutters (in holiday shapes,
   if available)
glue
markers
hole puncher

★ **Materials:**
red felt
sequins (or glitter)
short length of ribbon

Directions

1. Using marker, trace shape to be decorated around edge of cookie cutter.
2. Cut out shape, punch hole in top and thread ribbon through hole.
3. Dot felt with glue and decorate with sequins or glitter.

Paper Plate Rudolph

☆ **Tools:**
scissors
glue
pencil

 ★ **Materials:**
1 small paper plate
red and yellow construction
* paper scraps*
one sheet brown construction
paper

Directions

1. Draw, then cut with scissors, yellow circles for eyes, smaller brown circles for pupils, and a large red circle for Rudolph's nose.

2. Fold brown paper in half and draw large antler shape (accuracy not important).

3. Keeping paper folded, cut antlers with scissors.

4. Glue antlers, eyes and nose to paper plate.

5. Show children how placement of brown pupil inside yellow circle alters Rudolph's expression—each Rudolph should be a unique and personalized friend.

Paper Chain

☆ **Tools:**
scissors
glue

★ **Materials:**
1 sheet red construction paper
1 sheet green construction
* paper*

Directions

1. Cut paper into 1 inch by 4 inch strips.

2. Loop ends of paper strip together and secure with glue.

3. Loop second strip through first paper circle and secure ends with glue.

4. Alternate colors of red and green strips.

New Year's Hat and Noisemaker

☆ **Tools:**
scissors
glue

★ **Materials:**
toilet tissue tube
1 large sheet red construction
 paper
pieces of leftover Christmas
 wrapping paper
old stick-on bows
bits of ribbon
foil
used Christmas tinsel for decora-
 tions
1 small square waxed paper

Directions

New Year's Hat

1. Fold red paper in half, top to bottom.
2. Work with paper turned so that folded edge is at top.
3. Fold top left corner in to center of page.
4. Fold top right corner in to center of page.
5. Fold up remaining paper at the bottom of the hat on one side.
6. Turn hat over and fold up paper at the bottom of the other side.
7. Tuck a corner of this fold around the triangular crown section of the hat to help hold the hat together.
8. Secure with tape.
9. Turn the hat over and tuck the opposite corner around the triangular crown of the hat and tape. (This is a basic paper hat shape and can be used for all kinds of party hats, soldier hats and costumes.)
10. Tape or glue on ribbons to tie under the chin; glue ribbon bows and other decorations for trim.

Pine Cones

☆ **Tools:**
glue
glue brush

★ **Materials:**
pine cones
short lengths of ribbon
multicolored glitter

Directions

1. Tie ribbon around end of pine cone.
2. Brush with glue.
3. Sprinkle glitter over pine cone.

Note: If pine cones are difficult to obtain, small styrofoam balls or shapes cut from styrofoam egg carton tops can be used with very pretty results.

Noisemaker

1. Apply glue around one end of tissue roll.

2. Fold waxed paper square over end of tube and hold tightly, stretching waxed paper, until the glue adheres.

3. Cut a strip of decorative paper, such as foil Christmas wrap paper, the length of the tissue tube, and glue around the tube.

4. A piece of ribbon can be tied around the tube also, for an extra decoration.

5. When the glue is dry, hum into the open end of the noisemaker to make buzzing sound.

New Year's Bells

☆ **Tools:**
scissors
glue
crayons or makers

★ **Materials:**
1/2 sheet yellow construction
  paper
1/2 sheet red construction paper
glitter

Directions

1. Draw a big bell shape on the red paper, a slightly smaller bell shape on the yellow paper.
2. Cut out the shapes with scissors.
3. Write "Ring In the New!" on the yellow bell; "Ring Out the Old!" on the red bell.
4. Glue yellow bell on top the red bell with a small dot of glue near the top of the bell. Decorate "clapper" part of the bell with glue and glitter.

Cotton Puff Snowman in an Oatmeal Snowstorm

☆ **Tools:**
scissors
glue
black marker

★ **Materials:**
1 sheet black construction
  paper
3 cotton puffs
oatmeal (uncooked)
fabric scraps

Directions

1. Glue three cotton puffs to black paper to make a snowman.
2. Cut hat and scarf from fabric scraps and glue to snowman.
3. Draw dots for eyes, nose and buttons with black marker.
4. Apply glue to bottom of page, dot glue over the rest of the blacker paper and sprinkle with oatmeal so that it adheres to the glue.

Soap Paint Snowman

☆ **Tools:**
scissors
glue
paint brush
black crayon or maker

✱ ★ **Materials:**
white soap paint made with
*   white tempera (see page 124)*
1 sheet white construction paper
1 sheet colored construction
*   paper*
small red paper scrap
paint tray

Directions

1. Cut small, medium and large circles from white construction paper.
2. Glue in the shape of a snowman to the colored paper.
3. Cut a scarf from the red paper scrap (a rectangle with one frayed edge) and glue to snowman's neck.
4. Color features and buttons with black crayon.
5. Using paint brush, cover bottom of picture with thick globs of soap paint -apply very heavily.
6. Dot soap paint over the rest of the picture, especially on top the snowman's head and shoulders.

Nighttime Winter Picture

☆ **Tools:**
yellow crayon

★ **Materials:**
1 sheet black construction
*   paper*

Directions

1. Ask child to draw a familiar scene—a forest with animals, a house and garden, the school yard, a snow man —and use only the yellow crayon.
2. Explain that familiar things look very different at night—shadowy, dim, hazy (sometimes even scary) when there is little light; explain that it takes light to make colors.

Eskimo Sled and Dogs

☆ **Tools:**
scissors
tape
crayons or markers

★ **Materials:**
1/2 sheet brown construction
*   paper*
1/2 sheet black construction
*   paper*
12" piece of yarn

Directions

1. Fold 1/2 sheet black paper in half, lengthwise, to make sled.
2. Work with folded edge toward the top.
3. Draw a rectangle, with folded edge being top of shape.
4. Draw a long sled runner shape attached to bottom edge of rectangle, curving ends of runner up slightly.
5. Using scissors, cut along outside lines to cut out the sled—do not cut along folded edge.
6. Unfold the sled, fold the runners in, and the sled will stand on the runners.
7. Fold 1/2 sheet brown paper in half, lengthwise, to make the dogs.
8. Work with folded edge toward the top.
9. Draw two dogs - the back of the dog is the folded edge.
10. Dog's body can be a rectangle with a big, curving tail; head is half an oval shape, with a nose; legs can be short rectangles with rounded edges.
11. Use crayons to define dogs' faces and ears.
12. Cut around outside line of dog shapes.
13. When unfolded, they will also stand.
14. Tape yarn piece underneath dogs, one pulling the sled ahead of the other, and underneath sled.

Felt Fish

☆ **Tools:**
scissors
glue
markers

✱ ★ **Materials:**
"Fish colored" felt pieces (green, yellow, orange, purple)
construction paper scraps
collection of odd buttons or package of hole reinforcers

Directions

1. Draw fish shape on construction paper scrap to use for pattern.
2. Trace around fish shape on felt and cut with scissors.
3. Draw scales and fins on the felt with markers.
4. Glue hole reinforcer or button for fish's eye.
5. Glue felt shape to construction paper shape.
6. Optional: Packages of small magnets can be found easily and inexpensively used for projects.
7. If a magnet is glued to the back of the fish, a game can be played using a branch for a fishing pole, a piece of yarn for the fishing line, and another magnet tied to the end of the line. Explain how the Eskimos fished through the ice.
8. The fish can also be used as refrigerator door magnets.

Skis

☆ **Tools:**
crayons

★ **Materials:**
lengths of cardboard cut 5" x 24"
two yarn pieces, 8" long

Directions

1. Color cardboard skis on one side only.
2. Tie to shoes with yarn pieces.
3. Take the children on a "cross country" (down the hall) ski trip!

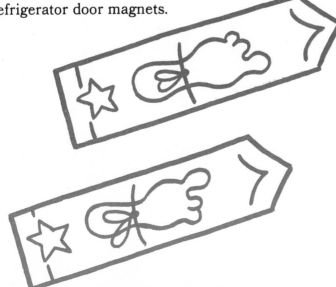

Snowstorm in a Jar

☆ **Tools:**
glue
crayons

★ **Materials:**
one baby food jar
snowman figure cut from
*   styrofoam egg carton top*
cotton puff
silver glitter
epoxy glue

SPECIAL PREPARATION NEED-
ED: Snowmen figures must be glued
to the lids of the baby food jars with
epoxy glue. Cut the snowman figures
out and ask the children to color eyes,
scarf and buttons with crayons. Adult
must secure figure to lid of jar with
epoxy, and it will take about five
minutes for the glue to set.

Directions
1. Fill the jar with water
2. Sprinkle about ¼ teaspoon silver
glitter into the water.
3. Screw on baby food jar lid tightly.
4. Cover lid with glue and glue on cotton puff, pulling the cotton puff
around to completely cover the metal
lid.
5. When the jar is turned upside
down, the glitter in the water will
drift down like snow—the cotton puff
represents a "snow drift" into which
the jar sits.

Earmuffs

☆ **Tools:**
glue
tape
crayons

★ **Materials:**
1 white construction paper strip
*   1" x 18"*
2 white paper circles, about 3" in
*   diameter*
1 3 foot length of yarn
tape
cotton puffs

Directions
1. Decorate headband strip with
crayons.
2. Glue one white circle to each end of
headband strip.
3. Lay yarn across underside of paper
pieces and tape to secure.
4. Cover circles with glue and glue
cotton puffs to outside of earmuff
circles.

Winter Hat

☆ **Tools:**
scissors
glue
crayons

★ **Materials:**
1 sheet colored construction
  paper
bits of ribbon
styrofoam packing pieces
yarn pom pom
colored stick-on stars
cereal
small hard candies or any other
  materials available for
  decoration

Directions

1. Draw a large stocking cap shape on the colored construction paper, and cut out this shape with scissors.
2. Decorate with crayons, glue and scrap materials collected for this purpose.

Mittens

☆ **Tools:**
scissors
glue
crayons
hole puncher

★ **Materials:**
☆ **Tools:**
1/2 sheet green construction
  paper
short length of yarn
1/2 sheet red construction paper
two cotton puffs

Directions

1. Trace around left hand on green paper and cut mitten shape out with scissors.
2. Trace around right hand on red paper and cut with scissors.
   (This is a good time to reinforce "left hand/right hand" lesson with younger children.)
3. Cover cuff of each mitten with glue and cotton puff.
4. Punch hole near edge of cuff and tie mittens together with length of yarn.
5. Make designs on mittens with crayons.

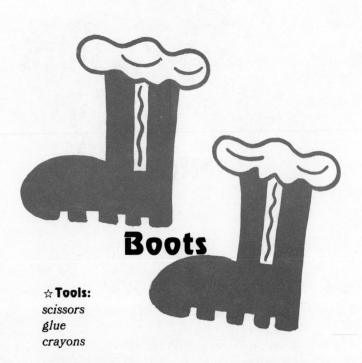

Boots

Winter Jacket

☆ **Tools:**
scissors
glue
crayons

☆ **Tools:**
scissors
glue

★ **Materials:**
1 sheet yellow or brown construction paper
strip of aluminum foil ½" x 6"
small black paper scrap
cotton puffs

★ **Materials:**
1 sheet colored construction paper
3" length of ric-rac tape or ribbon
cereal
small candies
bits of yarn
ribbons or assortment of odd buttons for decorations

Directions

1. Draw a boot shape on the brown paper and cut with scissors.
2. Glue strip of aluminum foil down the middle (zipper).
3. Cut a small triangle from the scrap of black paper and glue to top of aluminum strip (zipper tab).
4. Glue cotton puffs to top edge of boot.
5. Use crayons to outline foil and color sole at bottom of boot.

Directions

1. Draw shape of jacket on construction paper (simple shape: large rectangle body, two long rectangle arms, cut "v" shape for collar).
2. Cut out jacket with scissors.
3. Glue ric-rac or ribbon down middle of jacket, beginning at neckline.
4. Glue on candy "buttons" (or real buttons) and other material for jacket design.

Claydough Snowman

☆ **Tools:**
glue

★ **Materials:**
claydough (see page 124)
cookie decorations
2" length of ribbon
small twigs

Directions

1. Shape three small balls from claydough.
2. Glue one on top the other to build snowman.
3. Press cookie decorations into the head shape, then glue the head to the snowman's body.
4. Press cookie decorations into the body for buttons.
5. Tie ribbon around neck for scarf.
6. Press twigs into sides for arms.
7. Set aside to dry overnight.

City-Scape with Alphabet Snow

☆ **Tools:**
scissors
glue

★ **Materials:**
sheets of newspaper
box of alphabet noodles
1 sheet of black construction paper

Directions

1. Cut different sized rectangles and squares (some shapes can have domed or triangle shaped roofs) from the newspaper.
2. Turn black construction paper on the side and glue newspaper buildings along bottom edge.
3. Collage one shape over another to give depth to the picture.
4. Dot sky with glue and sprinkle alphabet noodle "snow" over the picture.

Jack in the Box

☆ **Tools:**

scissors
glue
crayons or markers

★ **Materials:**

1/2 sheet color construction
*   paper*
small white construction paper
*   scrap*
1" x 3" strip construction paper

Directions

1. Draw a small figure on the white construction paper scrap and color face, clothes, shoes with crayons or markers.

2. Cut out shape with scissors.

3. Bend paper strip back and forth in fan shape—this is the spring that will hold Jack in his box.

4. Glue one end of the paper spring to the back of the little figure.

5. Fold half sheet of construction paper in half.

6. Glue other end of paper spring to the inside of the folded sheet (the box).

7. When the glue is dry, push Jack down on his paper spring and close the box.

8. When the box is open, Jack will pop out.

Tissue Snowflakes

☆ **Tools:**

scissors
paint brush

★ **Materials:**

white tissue paper (or other thin
*   paper, easily cut when folded,*
*   such as typing paper)*
2 sheets waxed paper
liquid starch
iron

Directions

1. Cut tissue paper into 5" circles.

2. Fold in half, then fold in thirds.

3. Cut designs in the edges of the folded paper.

4. Unfold snowflakes.

5. Paint liquid starch over one piece of the waxed paper, and cover with second sheet of waxed paper.

6. Press with hot iron (over newspaper) to seal waxed paper edges.

7. Optional frame: Cut a large rectangle from the center of a piece of construction paper and glue to edges of waxed paper.

Chinese New Year Paper Lantern; Paper Plate Dragon

☆ **Tools:**
scissors
stapler
hole puncher
crayons

★ **Materials:**
*1 sheet orange construction
  paper*
2 small paper plates
*red and yellow construction
  paper scraps*
short length of yarn

Directions

LANTERN

1. Fold orange paper in half, lengthwise.
2. Starting at folded edge, make cuts about an inch apart to within one inch of edge of paper.
3. Unfold and staple edges of paper together, top to bottom.
4. Punch holes at either side of top of lantern and thread yarn through for handle.

DRAGON

1. Cut two paper plates in half.
2. Staple one half plate to another half plate, side by side to form a dragon's humped back.
3. Cut two small half circles from these centers to form top of head and jaw.
4. Staple one half-plate rim (curving upward) to one side of dragon's body to form the neck.
5. Staple the other half-plate rim to the other side of the dragon's body (curving downward) to form the dragon's tail.
6. Cut the end of the tail so that it forms a point.
7. Put the two small half circles that form the head together and staple onto the neck so that the mouth appears open.
8. With yellow paper scraps, cut two long triangles for teeth; with red paper, cut a long forked tongue.
9. Glue the tongue and teeth to the back of the dragon's head so that they show from the front.
10. Color the dragon green.

Snowball Banks

☆ **Tools:**
popsicle stick
masking tape

★ **Materials:**
styrofoam cup
1 penny
thick flour and water paste

Directions

1. Wrap masking tape across open end of cup to form the bottom of the snowball bank.
2. Turn cup over and, using popsicle stick, punch a slit in the cup so money can be inserted.
3. With hands, mold the thick flour and water mixture over the cup so that it is completely covered on all sides and top.
4. Use the popsicle stick as a tool to make swirls and peaks in the flour.
5. Insert the penny in the slot to keep the hole open while the flour paste dries (overnight).
6. The bank can be painted with white tempera after the flour dries to make the bank look more like a snowball.
7. To remove money, cut the tape at the bottom.

Stand-Up Snowman

☆ **Tools:**
scissors
glue

★ **Materials:**
large white construction paper
* scrap*
small black construction paper
* scrap*
1/2 sheet colored construction
* paper*
cotton puffs

Directions

1. Cut three strips, about 1" x 6", from the white paper.
2. Cut a hat shape from the black paper scrap.
3. Form each strip of white paper into a circle and secure with glue.
4. Stand one circle up on its side and glue to 1/2 sheet of construction paper.
5. Turn second circle on its side and glue to top of first circle.
6. Glue third circle to top of middle circle.
7. Work slowly—give each piece time to dry before continuing.
8. Glue cotton puffs to surface of 1/2 sheet of construction paper—this is the snow covered ground around the snowman.
9. Glue black hat to the top circle.

Winter Forest Scene

☆ **Tools:**
pencil

★ **Materials:**
*small evergreen branches cut
    into 3 or 4 inch pieces
    (Christmas tree trimmings or
    other outdoor greenery such
    as twigs or bush trimmings)
1 can spray snow (commercial
    flocking product easily found
    and inexpensive during the
    holiday season)
1 styrofoam or cardboard egg
    carton top
silver glitter*

Directions

1. Turn egg carton cover upside down to form base for winter scene.
2. Punch holes with pencil and insert tree trimmings to cover the top.
3. Spray branches and carton base with canned "snow"—sprinkle silver glitter over entire forest scene.
4. This is a beautiful and dramatic holiday table decoration—one can of spray snow is enough for a group of 20.

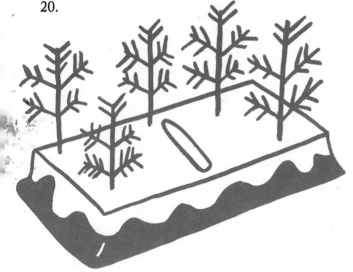

Ground Hog

☆ **Tools:**
*scissors
glue
crayons
paint brush*

★ **Materials:**
*styrofoam cup
popsicle stick
brown tempera paint mixed
    with 1/4 cup liquid detergent
small scrap brown construction
    paper
paint tray*

Directions

1. With scissors, cut an oval shape from the brown paper, small enough to fit inside the paper cup.
2. Draw features on the shape—face, small tail, paws—to represent the ground hog.
3. Punch hole in bottom of paper cup with popsicle stick.
4. Glue one end of the popsicle stick to the back of the ground hog shape.
5. With tempera/liquid detergent mixture, paint the styrofoam cup brown.
6. When the paint is dry, insert the popsicle stick into the cup.
7. The ground hog pops out of the "hole" when the popsicle stick is pushed through the cup.

Shadow Picture

☆ **Tools:**
scissors
tape
pencil

★ **Materials:**
1 sheet white construction
* paper*
1 sheet black construction
* paper*

Directions

1. Fold each sheet of construction paper in half, top to bottom, and cut along fold line to divide in halves.
2. On 1/2 sheet white paper, draw an animal, figure or shape.
3. Place this paper over 1/2 sheet of black paper and cut out the figure, cutting both sheets at once.
4. Glue the figure cut from the white paper to the bottom of the 1/2 sheet of black paper.
5. Glue the figure cut from black paper upside down and at the top edge of the 1/2 sheet of white paper.
6. Put the two half sheets together so that the black shape appears to be the shadow of the white figure, and tape the pieces together. (This shadow picture will help reinforce the lessons of light/dark relationship, the ground hog shadow story, etc.)

Heart Shaped Pins

☆ **Tools:**
tape
paint brush

★ **Materials:**
claydough
liquid red tempera paint
cookie sheet
safety pin
paint tray

Directions

1. Divide claydough into small balls and pat each claydough ball into a heart shape.
2. Bake on cookie sheet (250° for 1/2 hour), or leave overnight to dry.
3. Paint with red paint.
4. Tape safety pin to back when dry.

Valentine Frog

☆ **Tools:**
scissors
glue
pencil

★ **Materials:**
1/2 sheet red construction paper
1/2 sheet purple construction
  paper
1/2 sheet black construction
  paper

Directions

1. Fold the red paper in half and draw half a heart shape, with folded edge being center of the heart.
2. Cut along this curving line with scissors.
3. Cut two large circles from the purple paper.
4. Fold the black paper in half and draw half a wide, flat heart shape.
5. This shape should extend from the folded edge to the open edge, and be about 2" along the folded edge (from center of heart to point).
6. Keeping paper folded, cut out this wide heart shape.
7. Cut a small triangle into the bottom of the heart shape near the point, to form the frog's feet.
8. Cut two small circles from the remaining scraps of black paper.
9. Glue purple circles at top of red heart for eyes.
10. Glue small black circles inside the purple ones.
11. Glue the black heart foot shape to the back of the red heart at the bottom.

Valentine Cards

☆ **Tools:**
scissors
glue
pencil

★ **Materials:**
1 sheet red or pink construc-
  tion paper
available trims, such as: glitter,
  ribbons, doilies, wrapping
  paper, cotton puffs, sequins,
  stick-on stars, small candy
  hearts

Directions

1. Cut a large heart from the construction paper.
2. Decorate and personalize with available trims.
3. Messages can be written on the face of the heart or inside, using the folded heart as the card.
4. This is a free form exercise and children should be encouraged to use their own creativity.

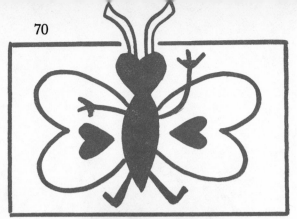

Valentine Butterfly

Abraham Lincoln's Birthday Card (February 12)

☆ **Tools:**
scissors
glue
black crayon or marker

★ **Materials:**
1 sheet yellow construction
* paper*
1 sheet red construction paper
black construction paper scrap
pipe cleaner

Directions

1. Fold red paper in half and cut along folded line.
2. Fold 1/2 sheet red paper in half, draw half heart shape and cut with scissors.
3. Using this heart as a pattern, trace around curving edge and draw another heart shape on the other 1/2 sheet red paper.
4. Cut this heart with scissors.
5. Cut a large oval shape from black paper scrap.
6. Place red hearts sideways on yellow construction paper, point to point, and glue.
7. Glue black oval (butterfly body) over red paper heart points, in center of page.
8. Cut a small heart shape from red paper scraps and glue to top of black oval for butterfly's head.
9. Bend pipe cleaner in half and glue to small heart head shape for antenna.
10. Legs and eyes and other features can be drawn on the butterfly with the black marker.

☆ **Tools:**
scissors
glue
crayons or markers

★ **Materials:**
1 sheet blue construction
* paper*
1/2 sheet white construction
* paper*
1/2 sheet red construction paper
3" x 3" square aluminum foil
black and brown construction
* paper scraps*
1 penny

Directions

1. Fold sheet of blue paper in half to make the card.
2. Cut about 1" off the edges of the white paper; cut about 2" off the edges of the red paper.
3. Glue white sheet in the center of the front of the card; glue red sheet in the center of the white sheet.
4. Place the aluminum foil over the penny and rub a finger over the foil to make the impression on the foil.
5. Move the penny around and make several impressions of Lincoln's head and the Lincoln Memorial on the back of the penny.
6. Carefully glue the piece of aluminum foil to the center of the card.
7. Message can be written at the top or inside the card.
8. Use the black and brown paper scraps to cut a tall, black hat or log cabin shape to further decorate the card.

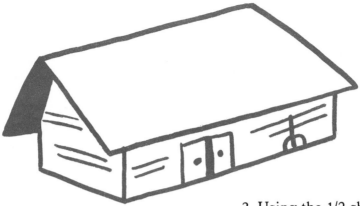

3-Dimensional Lincoln Log Cabin

☆ **Tools:**
scissors
glue
tape
markers

★ **Materials:**
1 sheet manila paper for cabin
  pattern
1 sheet brown construction
  paper
1 sheet black construction
  paper

Note: This is a project that requires more time, manual dexterity (and patience!) than the simpler, alternative log cabin project described below. Review the instructions to determine if the child is up to the challenge. The results are very rewarding!

Directions

1. Fold manila paper in half, lengthwise. Cut on folded line.
2. Using half sheet of manila paper, fold again lengthwise and cut on folded line. (You now have one 1/2 length of manila paper, and two ¼ lengths of manila paper.)

3. Using the 1/2 sheet of manila, fold at center so that it forms a square.
4. Draw a large triangle and cut it out, keeping paper folded. (You now have two triangles.)
5. Tape one triangle to each end of the top edge of one of the 1/4 length pieces of manila. This is the basic cabin pattern.
6. Discard all other manila paper scraps.
7. Fold brown construction paper in half, lengthwise. Trace manila cabin pattern onto brown paper and cut out this shape, keeping paper folded.
8. To assemble the cabin: Lay brown paper pieces side by side, and move the paper so that one triangular piece lies over the other in the middle. Glue these two middle pieces together. Fold the paper around forming four sides, and glue the two triangular pieces together at the front. (Your cabin now has a peaked, triangular roof at front and back, with short, rectangular sides.) Cut through both pieces at front to make a door that folds open.
9. For the roof, fold the black paper sheet in half, lay it over the top of the cabin, and glue or tape to secure.
10. With marker, draw horizontal lines representing logs. Draw windows, chimney, shutters, etc., on the cabin.

Alternate Lincoln Log Cabin Project

☆ **Tools:**
scissors
glue
crayons or markers

★ **Materials:**
large brown grocery bag, cut
into pieces
1 sheet colored construction
paper

Directions

1. Draw a large square in the center of the construction paper.
2. Draw a triangle on top for a roof.
3. Cut or tear brown paper bag into strips about 1" wide and the length of the house shape.
4. "Build" the log cabin by gluing the brown paper strips onto the shape.
5. The strips should be torn shorter as the roof narrows into the peak at the top.

Stethescope

☆ **Tools:**
scissors
glue
pencil

★ **Materials:**
1 sheet black construction
paper
1 small (2" square) piece
aluminum foil

Directions

1. Fold paper in half, lengthwise.
2. Draw a long, semi-circular line from top to bottom.
3. Draw another line about one inch inside the first one.
4. Keeping paper folded, cut along both lines so that two curved pieces (the stethescope "tubes") are cut at once.
5. Put the pieces together so that they form a circular shape and glue ends together at the bottom only. (The open ends of the two pieces are left unglued so that stethescope can fit over the head and rest around the neck.)
6. Cut a 3" shape from black paper scrap and glue on top of the two joined pieces.
7. Glue aluminum foil circle or square over the shape to complete the stethescope.

Note: The heart beat can actually be heard by placing a cardboard paper towel tube over the heart, if a real stethescope is not available for demonstration.

Valentine Treat Bag

☆ **Tools:**
scissors
glue
crayons

⭐ ★ **Materials:**
small brown paper bag
1 sheet red construction paper
pink or white construction paper
scraps

Directions

1. Fold sheet of red paper in half.
2. Draw small half heart shape and large half heart shape.
3. Cut hearts with scissors.
4. Cut four small hearts from pink or white paper scraps.
5. Cut four red paper strips from remaining piece of construction paper—about 1" by 5".
6. Fold these strips back and forth as in making a fan, to make springs for arms and legs.
7. Glue large red heart upside down in center of paper bag.
8. Glue smaller red heart, point to point, to make head for Valentine person.
9. Glue each little pink or white heart to one end of each red spring.
10. Glue the springs at arm and leg positions on Valentine person.
11. Draw features and other decorations on the bag with crayons.

Pretzel Stick Log Cabin

☆ **Tools:**
glue
crayons

⭐ ★ **Materials:**
1/4 sheet black construction paper, cut into triangle
1 sheet colored construction paper
bag of pretzel sticks

Directions

1. Glue black triangle roof to top of construction paper, point facing up.
2. Working down, "build" the log cabin using glue to hold pretzel sticks in place.
3. Also build pretzel stick chimney.
4. Use crayons to add details.

Cherry Tree

☆ **Tools:**
scissors
glue

✴ ★ **Materials:**
*1 sheet green construction
  paper*
*1 brown construction paper
  scrap*
*1 sheet colored construction
  paper for backing sheet*
*box of small cinnamon candies,
  or cookie decorations*

Directions

1. Cut green paper into 2" squares.
2. Cut rectangular tree trunk shape from brown paper scrap.
3. Glue brown tree trunk to construction paper backing sheet.
4. Cut green paper into small squares and glue overlapping shapes around top of tree trunk.
5. Glue on red cherry candies.

Paper Mache Cherries, Silver Coins for Delaware Game

☆ **Tools:**
scissors
tape
pencil

✴ ★ **Materials:**
facial tissues
flour and water paste
paste containers
pipe cleaners
plastic lid, any size
*aluminum foil sheet large
  enough to cover plastic lid*

*For game: Length of brown
  cloth, scarf or muffler*
*basket or circle cut from large
  piece of construction paper*

Directions

1. To make cherries, soak tissues in flour and water paste, and roll into balls.
2. Cut pipe cleaners in half.
3. Insert the end of each pipe cleaner piece into tissue ball.
4. Set aside to dry overnight.
5. To play Delaware game, cover plastic lid with aluminum foil piece.
6. Use pencil to add details—Washington's face, dollar sign, numbers—to make the lid look like a silver coin.
7. Lay brown cloth (the muddy Delaware river) on the floor.
8. Stand on one side and toss the coin across, trying to hit the basket or paper circle.
9. Prizes for hitting the basket could be a small, cherry candy.

Paint Paper Mache Cherries; Hatchet

☆ **Tools:**
glue
paint brush

★ **Materials:**
plastic or paper straw
small black construction paper
  scrap
red and brown paint
paint container
short length of yarn

Directions

1. Paint cherries with red paint.
2. Paint pipe cleaner stems brown.
3. Tie together in bunches with yarn.
4. Cut black paper into rectangle shape, 2" x 4".
5. Fold in half and cut open edges into hatchet shaped curve.
6. Fold over end of straw and glue in place.

George Washington

☆ **Tools:**
scissors
glue
paint brush
pencil

★ **Materials:**
spring type clothespin
1/4 sheet blue construction paper
1/4 sheet white construction
  paper
cotton puff
small piece of yarn
blue tempera paint
paint tray
gold or silver stick-on star

Directions

1. Paint clothespin blue, and stand it up so it will dry evenly.
2. Draw a circle (2" diameter) on the blue paper, and cut with scissors.
3. Inside the circle, draw a triangle.
4. Fold sides of circle up on these lines to form a 3-cornered hat.
5. Draw a small circle (1" diameter) on the white paper, and cut with scissors.
6. Cut two narrow strips from white paper (about 1" long).
7. Cross these strips in an "X" shape and glue together.
8. Draw a face on the small white circle.
9. Glue gold star in center of the "X".
10. Tie yarn around center of cotton puff and make a bow.
11. Glue hat on top of clothespin, point facing front.
12. Glue face and "X" shape to front of clothespin.
13. Glue cotton puff ponytail to back, under the hat.

Valentine Cat

☆ **Tools:**

scissors
glue
pencil

★ **Materials:**

paper cup
1/2 sheet red construction paper
small scrap white construction
  paper
small piece "curling" ribbon, or
  pipe cleaners or broomstraw
package of hole reinforcers

Directions

1. Fold red construction paper in half.
2. Draw one half large heart shape on fold, and four small heart shapes.
3. Cut and unfold.
4. Fold white paper scrap in half.
5. Draw two small heart shapes.
6. Cut and unfold.
7. Turn paper cup upside down—this is the cat's body.
8. Glue large red heart to front of cup, near the top.
9. Glue two small white hearts at top of red heart for ears.
10. Glue two red hearts, one above the other, to the front of the paper cup.
11. Glue two red hearts sticking out from under the front of the cup for feet.
12. Curl ribbon with scissors (or use pipe cleaner pieces or broomstraw) and glue these whiskers onto cat's face.
13. Use hole reinforcers for eyes—cut one hole reinforcer in half and glue on for cat's mouth.
14. Cut a curving tail from remaining red paper scraps and glue to back of cat.

Valentine Dog

☆ **Tools:**

scissors
glue
black crayon or marker

★ **Materials:**

1 sheet purple construction
  paper
1 sheet red construction paper

Directions

1. Fold sheet of purple paper in half, lengthwise.
2. Draw two heart shapes on the fold and cut with scissors.
3. Fold sheet of red paper in half, lengthwise.
4. Draw two small heart shapes for eyes; draw three long, thin heart shapes for ears and tongue; draw one short, fat heart shape for nose. Cut and unfold.
5. To assemble pieces for dog's face: Turn one purple heart upside down and glue over the top of the other purple heart, in hourglass shape.
6. Glue one long, thin heart shape (upside down) to back of upside down purple heart for tongue.
7. Glue on hearts for eyes, nose and ears.
8. Color in pupils, outline ears, and make dots for whiskers around dog's nose.

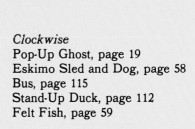

Valentine Fish

Valentine Mouse

☆ **Tools:**
scissors
glue
black crayon or marker

★ **Materials:**
1/2 sheet red construction paper
1/2 sheet white construction
   paper
red glitter
pieces of broomstraw

Directions

1. Fold red paper in half and draw one large heart shape and two smaller heart shapes. Cut and unfold.
2. On folded edge of white paper, draw one large heart shape and one small heart shape. Cut and unfold.
3. Cut long red paper tail.
4. To assemble pieces for mouse: Glue white heart to top of red heart (both points down).
5. Glue small red heart ears to white heart.
6. Glue red tail to back of mouse.
7. Glue small white heart to the end of the tail.
8. Glue broomstraw whiskers in place.
9. Draw circles for eyes, two tiny rectangles for teeth under the whiskers.
10. Dot eyes with glue and glitter.

☆ **Tools:**
scissors
glue
black marker

★ **Materials:**
1/2 sheet red construction paper
1/2 sheet white construction
   paper

Directions

1. Fold red paper in half and draw one large heart shape. Cut and unfold.
2. Fold white paper and draw two large hearts, one medium sized heart, and one small heart. Cut and unfold.
3. To assemble pieces for fish: Turn red heart sideways—point of heart is the fish's nose.
4. Turn both large white hearts sideways—points facing the same way as the fish's nose—and glue to top and bottom of red heart shape.
5. Glue medium sized heart—point facing nose—in between the two large white hearts.
6. Glue small white heart for eye.
7. Use black marker to detail scales, fins, and fish's mouth.

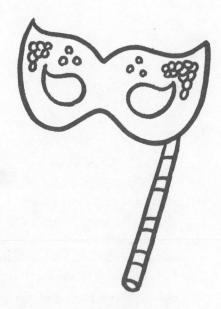

Mardi Gras Mask

☆ **Tools:**
scissors
glue or tape
crayons or markers

★ **Materials:**
2 plastic or paper straws
1/2 sheet colored construction
    paper
small piece cellophane or plastic
    wrap

Directions

1. On construction paper, draw a mask or eyeglass shape.
2. Cut out this shape and cut holes for eyes.
3. Decorate with markers, glue and glitter.
4. Slip one straw inside the other to make one long straw.
5. Tape to side of mask.
6. Tape cellophane or plastic wrap across eye holes in back of mask.

Tall Black Lincoln Hat

☆ **Tools:**
scissors
tape or stapler

★ **Materials:**
2 sheets black construction
    paper
1/2 sheet black construction
    paper cut lengthwise

Directions

1. Tape two whole sheets of black paper together, at the short sides.
2. Wrap around head to fit, and tape or staple together to form tall black tube shape.
3. Tape 1/2 sheet black paper across the front to make the brim.

Bean and Macaroni Wall Hanging

☆ **Tools:**
glue
pencil

★ **Materials:**
styrofoam meat or vegetable
  tray
short length of yarn
five different dried beans and
  noodles
suggestions: elbow macaroni,
  egg noodles, spinach noodles,
  dried peas, dried lima beans,
  alphabet noodles, dried kidney
  beans

Directions

1. With pencil draw a large "M" in the meat tray, dividing the tray into five equal sections.
2. Cover each section with glue, one at a time.
3. Cover each section with a different dried bean or noodle.
4. Punch two holes in the top of the meat tray.
5. Thread yarn through holes and tie.

George Washington Hat

☆ **Tools:**
paint brush
stapler

★ **Materials:**
large, double size sheet of
  newspaper
red, white and blue tempera
  paint
paint trays
can of hair spray or spray starch

Directions

1. Fold large sheet of newspaper at the already pre-folded line to strengthen hat shape.
2. Work with paper turned so that folded edge is at top.
3. Fold hat as described in *New Year's Hat and Noisemaker* on page 54.
4. Staple open end (bottom) of hat near front and back to keep the hat together—also staple at top of triangular crown.
5. Paint newspaper hat with red, white and blue stripes.
6. When paint dries, spray with hair spray or spray starch to fix paint and prevent it from rubbing off.

March Lion Mask

☆ **Tools:**
scissors
crayons

✳ ★ **Materials:**
1 large brown grocery bag

Directions
1. Work with bag open end down.
2. Pull away half the section sealing the closed end of the bag, and cut two triangle ears to stand up.
3. Cut two large holes in front of the back, near the top, to see through when the bag is worn over the head.
4. Cut a large mouth with big triangular teeth.
5. Fringe the front edge of the bag with 4" cuts to look like the lion's mane.
6. Draw whiskers and nose, outline eyes, and draw ears and mane with crayons.

Plastic Bread Bag Kite

☆ **Tools:**
tape or stapler

✳ ★ **Materials:**
large plastic bread bag
2-3' length of yarn
long 1" strip of wrapping paper
brown paper bag, or construc-
tion paper scrap

Directions
1. Staple or tape yarn to open edge of plastic bag.
2. Fold paper strip back and forth as in making a fan or spring.
3. Staple one end to bottom, closed end of bag.
4. When the plastic bag fills with air it will soar up into the air.

Windmill Picture

☆**Tools:**
scissors
crayons

✳ ★**Materials:**
*1 sheet colored construction
    paper*
*1/2 sheet yellow construction
    paper*
1 small metal brad

Directions
1. Cut the ½ sheet yellow paper into a rectangle.
2. Either cut the top of the triangle into a point, or round off into a dome shape.
3. Glue the rectangle to the sheet of construction paper, positioning it vertically.
4. Cut two small rectangular strips from the yellow paper scraps, about 1" x 6".
5. Cross them into an "X" and secure to the top of the windmill shape with the metal brad so that the windmill blades can turn.
6. Draw large "X's" over the body of the windmill and use crayons to add other details.

March Lion

☆**Tools:**
scissors
glue
crayons

★**Materials:**
*1 sheet yellow construction
    paper*
*1/2 sheet orange construction
    paper*
*short lengths of black or brown
    yarn (for whiskers and tail)*

Directions
1. Fold yellow paper in half, top to bottom.
2. Cut a 3" circle from center of paper at the bottom of unfolded edges.
3. Cut a 5" circle from the orange paper and fringe the edges with scissors.
4. Glue the orange circle to one corner of the folded edge of yellow paper.
5. Glue one yellow circle in the center of the orange circle.
6. Draw eyes, nose and mouth in the yellow circle.
7. Glue on whiskers.
8. Glue tail to other corner of the folded edge of yellow paper.
9. Use crayons to add details.
10. When unfolded, this lion will stand up.

Paper Kite Picture

☆ **Tools:**
scissors
glue

★ **Materials:**
1/2 sheet colored construction
   paper
1 sheet blue construction paper
length of yarn—about 2 feet
small squares of colored tissues
package of colored, stick-on stars

Directions

1. Using half sheet of colored paper, cut a kite shape (diamond shape).
2. Glue to upper part of the large sheet of paper.
3. Cut yarn into lengths to fit across paper kite, both horizontally and vertically.
4. Cut a short length for kite's tail.
5. Glue yarn pieces into kite picture.
6. Using remaining yarn piece, glue one end to center of kite, where the strings cross, and let the rest of the yarn dangle.
7. Twist tissue squares into bow shapes and glue to kite's tail.
8. Decorate kite with colored stars.

Telescope

☆ **Tools:**
scissors
glue
pencil
paint brush

★ **Materials:**
toilet tissue tube
1/2 sheet black construction
   paper
small piece of plastic food wrap
   (2" square)
black tempera paint
paint tray

Directions

1. Roll black paper into tube shape, small enough to fit (snugly) inside toilet tissue tube.
2. Use pencil to mark the place where the paper should be cut, and use scissors to cut black paper.
3. Glue overlapping edge of paper to form the telescope tube shape.
4. Paint toilet tissue tube with black paint.
5. When dry, apply glue to outside rim of one end of the tissue tube, stretch plastic wrap over this end, and hold in place until the glue adheres.
6. Slip the black paper tube inside the toilet tissue tube to complete the telescope.

Paper Plate Moon Clock

☆ **Tools:**
scissors
glue
crayons or markers

★ **Materials:**
1 large paper plate
red, black and yellow construction paper scraps
1 small metal brad
gold and silver stick-on stars

Directions
1. Cut two long rectangles from the black paper (clock's hands).
2. Cut two small red triangles and glue to the ends of the black hands.
3. Cut a large yellow semi-circle half-moon shape.
4. Glue the yellow moon on the paper plate.
5. Attach clock's hands to center of plate with metal brad.
6. Draw numbers at appropriate places around the edge of the paper plate.
7. Glue one star at the point of one red triangle—this is the "hour" hand.
8. Glue gold and silver stars to decorate the plate.

Rocket Ship to the Moon

☆ **Tools:**
scissors
glue
crayons

★ **Materials:**
1 sheet blue construction paper
1/2 sheet yellow construction paper

Directions
1. Cut a circle in the yellow construction paper and glue to upper corner of blue paper.
2. Cut a small rectangle with a triangle for nose cone of the rocket.
3. Glue this paper rocket shape at bottom of construction paper (aiming it toward the moon).
4. With crayons, draw flames coming from end of rocket, stars, comets, and other details.

Rocket Ship

☆ **Tools:**
scissors
glue

✱ ★ **Materials:**
toilet tissue cardboard roll
piece of aluminum foil
*1/2 sheet green construction
   paper (or foil wrapping paper)*
*4" square construction paper
   scrap*
*strip of red felt, cut 6" x 2" (or
   red construction paper, if felt
   not available)*

Directions

1. Cut green paper to fit around cardboard tube.
2. Glue around tube.
3. Roll 4" square into cone shape and secure with glue.
4. Cut a 4" square from the aluminum foil and roll around construction paper cone.
5. Secure with glue.
6. Push large end of the cone shape into the cardboard tube to form pointed nose cone of the rocket ship.
7. Cut strips of aluminum foil and glue to cardboard tube for detail.
8. Cut triangles out of one edge of the red felt (or red paper) to make flames.
9. Glue this jagged strip around inside of cardboard tube at the open end.

"The Moon is Made of Green Cheese" and Crackers Party; Paper Bag Rocket

☆ **Tools:**
bowl
spoon
knife for spreading cheese

✱ ★ **Materials:**

large package of cream cheese
green food coloring
crackers
small brown paper bag
balloon

Directions

1. Cream a few drops of green food coloring into the cheese.
2. Spread on crackers and eat.
3. Explain the myth of the moon being made of green cheese, and how astrologers can now use the telescope to explore the heavens.
4. To make rocket: draw a picture of a rocket ship on the side of the brown paper bag (open end of bag toward the bottom).
5. Color with crayons.
6. Blow up the balloon and slip the bag over the balloon.
7. Release the balloon and watch the rocket shoot up into the air.

Bouncing Leprechaun

☆ **Tools:**
scissors
glue
crayons

★ **Materials:**
1 large sheet white construction
  paper
1 sheet green construction paper
length of yarn, green or white

Directions

1. Cut a large oval or round shape from the white paper.
2. Cut a large green derby hat to fit the white paper oval: half circle crown, rectangle brim.
3. Cut four 1" strips from the green paper and fold back and forth as in making fan or spring shape.
4. Glue the hat to the top of the leprechaun's head.
5. Glue the green springs at sides of head for arms, at bottom of head for legs.
6. Draw eyes, mouth, pipe in the mouth, shamrock shape on the hats, etc. for details.
7. Punch hole at top of hat, and hang this bouncing leprechaun from the ceiling by the piece of yarn.

St. Patrick's Day Pin (March 17)

☆ **Tools:**
scissors
glue
pencil

★ **Materials:**
1/4 sheet construction paper
  safety pin
2 small squares green and white
  tissue paper
gold glitter

Directions

1. To make a shamrock shape: fold green construction in half.
2. Draw three small heart shapes on the fold.
3. Cut out these hearts and glue together at the points.
4. Cut a small stem and glue to bottom of shamrock shape.
5. Crush green tissue and glue tissue ball to center of shamrock.
6. Crush white tissue and glue over center of green tissue.
7. Sprinkle gold glitter over a dot of glue in the center of the tissue.
8. Pin to shirt.

Rainbow and Pot O'Gold

☆ **Tools:**
scissors
glue
crayons

★ **Materials:**
1 sheet white construction paper
1/2 sheet yellow construction paper

Directions

1. Draw a pot of gold on the yellow paper (can be a half circle with three legs).
2. Cut out with scissors and glue to bottom of white construction paper.
3. Using crayons, draw a rainbow going into the pot o' gold.

Shamrock Shape Collage

☆ **Tools:**
scissors
glue
pencil

★ **Materials:**
1 sheet green construction paper
green tissue square, cut about 2" square
gold glitter

Directions

1. Draw shamrock shape on green paper (or use method described in *St. Patrick's Day Pin on page 85*).
2. Cut out shape and cover with glue.
3. Crush tissue squares and collage the shape.
4. Sprinkle with gold glitter.
5. Write child's name on the stem.

Celebrate Spring— Plant Birdseed (1st Day of Spring is March 21)

Leprechaun Man

☆ **Tools:**
scissors
glue
crayons

★ **Materials:**
1 sheet green construction paper
1 sheet white construction paper

Directions

1. On green paper draw large shamrock shape (or use cut and fold method) with a stem for leprechaun's neck.
2. Draw a circle.
3. Draw two small ovals for feet.
4. Draw a derby hat (half circle with rectangle brim).
5. Cut the pieces out with scissors.
6. Glue shamrock shape upside down on sheet of white paper.
7. Glue on circle head and hat.
8. With crayons, draw arms and legs.
9. Glue on oval shaped feet.
10. Add features and details with crayons.

☆ **Tools:**
spoon

★ **Materials:**
1 paper cup
birdseed
water
bag of garden soil or commercial potting soil

Directions

1. Spoon dirt into paper cup.
2. Poke finger into dirt.
3. Plant birdseed.
4. Water and place in shady area.
5. Birdseed will begin to show green within 2-3 days.

NOTE: For very dramatic results, place the paper cups on a tray, water thoroughly, and put the tray inside a large plastic garbage bag. This homemade greenhouse will keep the plants moist for the entire sprouting time, so the seeds won't have to be watered every day. Remove the plastic bag after 3 or 4 days—the children will be very surprised at how much the birdseed has grown!

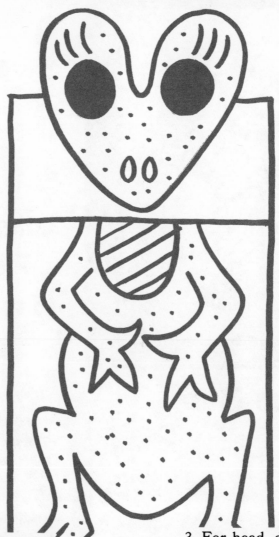

Paper Bag Frog Puppet

☆ **Tools:**
scissors
glue
crayons

★ **Materials:**
small brown paper bag
1 sheet green construction paper
1 red construction paper scrap

Directions

1. To cut frog shape: draw a large oval on green paper about the size of the paper bag.

2. Draw a triangle at each side of the bottom of the oval for feet.

3. For head, draw two large circles, connected by an oval shape about the size of the bottom of the bag.

4. Cut out these pieces with the scissors.

5. Work with closed end of paper bag facing up, (paper bag upside down).

6. Glue head piece to flap.

7. Under the flap, glue the body piece to the side of the paper bag.

8. Using red construction paper, cut a large oval tongue.

9. Glue the tongue over the body, and under the flap.

10. Draw eyes, arms, details with crayon.

11. Slip hand inside the bag, fingers inside the flap.

12. Wiggle fingers up and down to make the frog talk.

Paper Plate Turtle

☆ **Tools:**
scissors
glue
crayons
paint brush

★ **Materials:**
2 small paper plates
dried lima beans
1/2 sheet brown construction
  paper
brown tempera paint
paint tray

Directions

1. Turn one paper plate upside down and glue to the other, forming turtle's shell.
2. Paint with brown tempera.
3. While paint dries, draw turtle's head (oval), feet (rectangles with toes) and tail on brown paper.
4. Cut out these pieces and glue to underside of turtle's shell.
5. Dot top of shell with glue.
6. Glue on lima beans for shell's textured look. (Paint lima beans brown, if you wish.)

Sponge Paint Kite Shape

☆ **Tools:**
scissors
tape
sponge
pencil

★ **Materials:**
1 sheet red construction paper
1/2 sheet colored construction
  paper
12" length of yarn
tempera paint
paint tray

Directions

1. Draw kite shape on red paper.
2. Draw four bows for kite's tail on yellow paper (triangles joined at one point).
3. Cut out the paper pieces with scissors.
4. Tape one end of the yarn to the bottom of the kite, and tape bows to the yarn.
5. Using sponge, paint kite and bows.

NOTE: Another fun way to make designs on the kite is to use your thumb instead of a sponge!

Lamb with Cotton Puffs

☆ **Tools:**
scissors
glue

✱★ **Materials:**
1 sheet white construction paper
cotton puffs
styrofoam packing material if
  available
blue, black, and pink construc-
  tion paper scraps

Directions

1. Fold white paper in half, lengthwise.
2. Cut a 3" circle from the center of the unfolded edges.
3. Use one circle for scrap paper.
4. From this, cut two oval ears, one large oval tail.
5. Glue ears on the other white circle.
6. Glue the circle to one corner of the folded edge of white paper (this is lamb's head).
7. Glue the tail to the other corner of the folded edge of white paper.
8. Cut round blue eyes, oval pink tongue, and hourglass shaped nose from black scraps.
9. Glue to lamb's head.
10. Cover one side of the lamb shape with glue.
11. Cover the shape with cotton puffs and styrofoam pieces.
12. When unfolded, this lamb will stand up.

Pistachio Pudding Finger Painting

☆ **Tools:**
bowl
spoon

 ★ **Materials:**
1 package instant pistachio pudding mix (use water instead of milk to mix)
fingerpaint paper

Directions

1. Mix pudding using a little less water than package directions call for.
2. Spoon pudding onto fingerpaint paper and use for fingerpaint.
3. Explain the symbolic use of the color green for St. Patrick's Day, that Ireland is called "The Emerald Isle", etc.
4. Draw a shamrock with one finger when finger play is over, and spread papers over tabletop to dry.

Moon Surface

 ☆ **Tools:**
bowl
spoon
popsicle stick

★ **Materials:**
6-7" circle of cardboard
flour
water

Directions

1. Mix flour and water into thick paste.
2. Spoon a portion onto the cardboard circle.
3. Use popsicle stick to make mountains and craters with the paste.

Wind Picture

☆ **Tools:**
scissors
glue
crayons

★ **Materials:**
2 twigs about 6" long, to use for clothesline poles
yarn piece, about 6" long, to use for clothesline
fabric pieces
1 sheet construction paper

Directions

1. Cut shirts, pants, skirts, from fabric pieces (use basic shapes with younger children).

2. Try to cut the clothing slightly askew, so that when "hung" on the clothesline, they will fall in a slight sideways direction, as if being blown by the wind. (You must cut all cloth pieces blowing in the same direction!)

3. Glue twig clothesline poles to each side of the construction paper backing sheet.

4. String yarn piece between poles and glue in place.

5. Glue the clothes to the clothesline by the top of each material piece only, so they will flap in the wind.

6. With crayons, draw background detail, such as trees bending in the wind, leaves blowing through the air, dark clouds, etc.

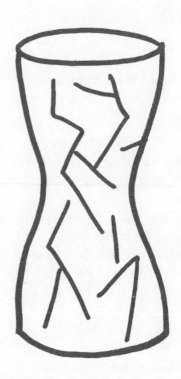

Passover Goblet

☆ **Tools:**
transparent tape

★ **Materials:**
2 paper cups
1 small piece of aluminum foil, 8" x 8"

Directions

1. Place paper cups bottom to bottom.

2. Tape together around middle.

3. Roll foil around both cups and crunch together to follow shape of cups.

4. Tape to hold foil.

Easter Basket and Cotton Puff Bunny in a Swing

☆ **Tools:**
scissors
glue

✱ ★ **Materials:**
EASTER BASKET:
plastic berry basket
2 10" pipe cleaners
8" square tissue paper

BUNNY:
ribbon or yarn 15" long
1 egg cup section cut from
   styrofoam egg container
cotton puff
confetti cookie decorations
bits of pink yarn for trim

Directions

EASTER BASKET
1. Attach one 10" pipe cleaner to each side of basket for handle.
2. Weave ribbon in and out sides of basket.
3. Glue end of ribbon to secure. Line with tissue.

BUNNY
1. Gently pull cotton puff to form head shape and pull cotton up for ears.
2. Glue on cookie decorations for eyes, nose, mouth.
3. Decorate ears and top of egg carton section with ribbon bits.
4. Poke pipe cleaner through sides of egg carton (bend inside to secure) to make the swing.
5. A drop of glue keeps the bunny in the swing.

Fuzzy Bunny

☆ **Tools:**
scissors
glue

✳ ★ **Materials:**
1 sheet pink construction paper
cotton puffs
black yarn
*small red candies for eyes and
   nose*

Directions

1. To draw bunny: Circle body, small circle for head, elongated ovals for ears, two horizontal ovals at bottom of circle body for feet.
2. Cut out bunny shape.
3. Cover bunny shape with glue.
4. Gently separate cotton puffs into a thin layer and glue cotton to bunny.
5. Add red candies and yarn whiskers with a drop of glue.

Bunny Ears Headband and Easter Egg Holder

☆ **Tools:**
scissors
glue
tape
crayons or markers

✳ ★ **Materials:**
*1 sheet purple construction
   paper*
1 sheet pink construction paper
*strip of white construction
   paper, 2" x 8"*
small square pink tissue paper
*small red candies for eyes and
   nose*
cotton puff
4 2" pieces of pipe cleaner
glitter

Egg Carton Duckling

☆ **Tools:**
scissors
glue

★ **Materials:**
yellow styrofoam egg carton section
orange and black construction paper scraps
yellow tissue paper scraps
small piece yellow yarn

Directions

1. Cut shapes for bill and feet from orange construction paper.
2. Cut small black circles for eyes.
3. Cut yellow tissue wing shapes, two for each side of baby duck.
4. Cut small pieces of yarn for top of head.
5. Glue paper pieces and yarn and tissue trims to egg carton section.

Directions

BUNNY EARS HEADBAND:

1. Cut two 2" strips from long edge of purple paper, measure to fit child's head and tape.
2. With marker, draw two bunny ear shapes on pink paper, cut with scissors, and tape ears to inside of headband.
3. Decorate with glue and glitter.

EASTER EGG HOLDER:

1. Tape ends of 2" white paper strip to form circle.
2. Cut pink ears from construction paper scraps.
3. Glue one pipe cleaner piece to outside middle of each ear.
4. Glue two pipe cleaner pieces for whiskers.
5. Glue crushed tissue ball for nose, red candies for eyes, and cotton puff in back for tail.
6. Mouth and other features can be drawn with markers.

Eggshell Picture

☆ **Tools:**
glue
crayons

 ★ **Materials:**
eggshells (for group of twenty
    children, about 3 dozen are
    needed), crushed into small
    pieces
food coloring
bowls (1 for each color used)
spoon
1 sheet pastel colored construc-
    tion paper

Directions

1. Using crayons, draw a large flower
(or several small ones) on the construction paper.
2. Put crushed eggshells into bowls,
add a few drops of food coloring in
each bowl, and toss with spoon to col-
or shells.
3. Cover flower picture with glue and
sprinkle with dyed eggshell.

Bunny in a Coat

☆ **Tools:**
scissors
glue
crayons or markers

★ **Materials:**
1 sheet pink construction paper
1 sheet blue construction paper
button

Directions

1. To draw bunny on pink paper,
follow directions given on page 94.
2. Cut out bunny shape.
3. To make bunny's coat, fold blue
paper in half, top to bottom.
4. Lay bunny shape on top of blue
paper, shoulders at folded edge.
5. Draw coat by tracing around bunny.
6. Keeping paper folded, cut out coat.
7. Do not cut on folded edge.
8. Cut open coat in front from collar to
hem.
9. Cut a "V" shaped wedge at collar.
10. Slip the coat over the shoulders of
the bunny.
11. Glue on button.
12. With markers, draw button hole
and features on bunny's face.

Raining "Cats and Dogs"

☆ **Tools:**
scissors
glue
crayons or markers

★ **Materials:**
1 sheet brown construction
  paper
cotton puffs
1 sheet blue or grey construction
  paper

Directions

1. To draw cats: oval body, circle head with triangle ears, elongated oval legs, long curving tail.
2. To draw dogs: oval body, circle head with floppy, oval ears, elongated oval legs, and oval tail.
3. Cut out shapes and glue to back sheet in the middle of the paper.
4. Gently separate cotton puffs and glue across top of page for clouds.
5. Draw in grass at bottom of page, and raindrops falling from clouds.

Chick in the Egg

☆ **Tools:**
scissors
glue
crayons or markers

★ **Materials:**
yellow and purple construction
  paper
brass brad
cookie decorations

Directions

1. With marker, draw a large oval shape on the purple construction paper with a zig-zag line dividing the egg in half.
2. Cut out the oval, and cut along the zig-zag line so that the eggshell is "broken" in half.
3. Draw a chick's head, beak and neck on the yellow paper, and cut this out.
4. Glue chick to inside bottom half of shell.
5. Attach top half of shell to bottom half with brass brad, so the shell can be opened and closed.
6. Decorate with cookie decorations.

Stand-up Bunny

☆ **Tools:**
scissors
glue
tape

★ **Materials:**
1 sheet pink construction paper
black yarn, felt, ribbon or scrap
  paper pieces for trim
cotton puff
toilet tissue cardboard roll

Directions

1. Fold pink paper in half, top to bottom.
2. Draw bunny shape as previously described on half sheet of paper.
3. Cut out both bunny shapes at once.
4. Glue or tape together at edges—do not tape bottom edge.
5. Cut eyes, nose, bow tie and other trims and whiskers.
6. Insert toilet tissue tube into bunny from the bottom and stand the bunny up.

Aquarium

☆ **Tools:**
glue
crayons

★ **Materials:**
1 sheet white construction paper
blue tissue paper cut same size
  as construction paper
spray bottle filled with water
Optional:
tiny seashells
pieces of green plants
fine sand (or yellow tempera
  mixed with salt)

Directions

1. Outline the edges of white construction paper with black crayon to emphasize aquarium shape.
2. Draw fish (realistic or imaginary), seahorses, starfish, octopus, plants, rocks, turtles, etc. in the aquarium.
3. If trims are used, glue to paper (apply glue along bottom of aquarium and sprinkle sand over the glue).
4. Lay blue tissue over the aquarium and spray with water.
5. When dry, carefully remove tissue.
6. The dye from the tissue paper will be transferred to the aquarium picture.

Panda Bear with Moveable Arms

☆ **Tools:**
scissors
glue
crayons or markers

★ **Materials:**
1 sheet grey construction paper
1 sheet black construction paper
2 small metal brads

Directions

1. On grey construction paper, draw Panda head (circle), two fat arms (ovals) and two fat leg shapes (ovals).
2. Cut out these shapes with scissors.
3. Draw a black circle or oval shape on the black paper (this will be the body of the bear), and cut out with scissors.
4. Glue legs to bottom of oval shape.
5. Glue grey head at top of the black oval.
6. Attach each arm to side of body with metal brad.
7. Draw features on the bear's face with markers. (Buttons, bows, ribbons or other trims can be added if available.)

Fold and Cut Puppy

☆ **Tools:**
scissors
glue
crayons

★ **Materials:**
1 sheet brown construction paper
short lengths of brown, black or white yarn
small scrap red construction paper

Directions

1. Fold brown paper in half, lengthwise.
2. Cut a circle (4" diameter) from center of paper—bottom of circle is at open edges of paper.
3. Glue one brown circle to upper corner of folded paper. (This is the puppy's head.)
4. Cut two long oval shapes from other brown circle and glue to head for ears.
5. Cut an oval from the red paper scrap and glue to head for tongue.
6. Glue yarn to other edge of folded paper for tail.
7. Color eyes, nose, spots or other features on the puppy with crayons.
8. When unfolded, this puppy will stand.

Chick in Eggshell

☆ **Tools:**
scissors
glue

✶ ★ **Materials:**
cotton puff
confetti cookie decorations
1 empty eggshell broken in half
green construction paper scraps
yellow tempera paint powder
saucer

Directions

1. Gently pull cotton puff to form head of chick.
2. Roll cotton lightly in saucer of yellow powdered paint to color chick yellow.
3. Cut pieces of green paper to make a nest, and glue these together to form base.
4. Place one half eggshell inside the other and secure with a drop of glue.
5. Glue eggshell to green paper base.
6. Put the chick in the egg, and glue on cookie decorations for eyes and beak.

Pussy Willow Picture

☆ **Tools:**
glue
crayons or markers

✶ ★ **Materials:**
cotton puffs
twigs
construction paper

Directions

1. Glue twigs to construction paper.
2. Pull cotton puffs in half, roll into balls, and glue to twigs.
3. Use crayons to draw detail work, such as a vase to hold the pussy willows.

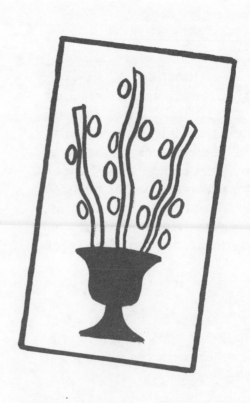

Watering Can Picture

☆ **Tools:**
scissors
glue
crayons

★ **Materials:**
1 sheet pastel blue construction paper
1 sheet colored construction paper or large wallpaper sample or sheet of gift wrap paper.

Directions

1. Draw a watering can on the colored paper, wallpaper sample or other paper used: large square with handle on one side, spout on the other.
2. Cut out this shape with scissors.
3. Glue to top of blue construction paper, with spout pointing down.
4. Draw water coming from the spout and flowers along bottom edge of blue paper.

Rainy Day Picture

☆ **Tools:**
scissors
glue
blue or black markers

★ **Materials:**
1 sheet blue construction paper
1/2 sheet any color construction paper (for umbrella shape)
1 sheet white construction paper
10" pipe cleaner
blue food coloring
spray bottle filled with water

Directions

1. Cut 1/2" off edges of white construction paper.
2. Lightly glue white paper to the blue sheet so that the picture will appear framed.
3. Draw an umbrella shape (half a large circle with triangles cut from flat edge) on half sheet of construction paper.
4. Cut out this shape with scissors.
5. Glue umbrella to paper around top edge of umbrella, pulling the center of the shape out and away from the backing sheet so that the umbrella appears three-dimensional.
6. Bend pipe cleaner at the bottom to form curved handle, and glue to page under the umbrella shape.
7. Cover umbrella and paper with blue marker raindrops.
8. Add a few drops food coloring to water in spray bottle, and spray picture. (The marker raindrops will blur and the white paper will turn a drizzly blue).

Paint a Pet Rock

☆ **Tools:**
paint brush

★ **Materials:**
large, smooth rock
2 colors paint
paint trays
container of water
clear enamel glaze

Directions

1. Paint rock with one color paint.
2. When dry (and it will dry quickly if tempera paint is used), add details such as eyes, stripes, spots, with another color paint.
3. The clear enamel glaze (available in spray can) should be applied by the teacher.
4. Enamel is not essential, but will give the rocks an attractive, shiny look, and the tempera will be "fixed" and will not rub off on children's hands.
5. Tempera can also be "fixed with spray starch.

Butterfly

☆ **Tools:**
scissors
pencil

★ **Materials:**
1 pastel colored sheet construc-
   tion paper
2" piece of plastic straw, slit
   down one side
colored chalk
spray starch
5" length of yarn

Directions

1. Fold construction paper in half, top to bottom.
2. Draw one half of butterfly's body and wing on folded sheet of construction paper (accuracy is not important here) with body on the fold.
3. Cut out shape and color in designs with chalk.
4. Punch a small hole midway down the fold of the butterfly with sharp point of pencil.
5. Thread yarn through the hole and tie.
6. Cut 2" piece of straw into two pieces, and push over paper fold on each side of the knot.
7. Gently unfold butterfly, bending paper in on each side of the straw, and spray with starch to fix chalk.
8. When the butterfly dries, the wings will curl up into a delicate shape, and when lifted by the yarn will seem to glide and flutter.

Caged Zoo Animal

☆ **Tools:**
scissors
glue
crayons

★ **Materials:**
*1 sheet construction paper back-
   ing, any color*
1 sheet black construction paper
1 sheet white construction paper

Directions

1. On white paper, draw a shapes animal.

2. Example: To draw an elephant, draw oval body; circle head—draw elephant's trunk also; large triangle ear; thick rectangle legs.

3. Cut black paper into six strips, about 1/2" x 8".

4. Cut out shape and glue to backing sheet.

5. With crayons, color shape and add details.

6. Glue strips of black paper to top and bottom of page for cage roof and floor.

7. Glue strips vertically for zoo bars.

NOTE: Pictures may also be cut from magazine and saved for this project.

Flowers Grow-ing in Green Grass

☆ **Tools:**
scissors
glue
crayons

★ **Materials:**
white construction paper sheet
*1/2 sheet green construction
   paper (cut lengthwise)*

Directions

1. Fringe green paper to resemble a strip of green grass.

2. Glue grass to bottom of white paper sheet.

3. With crayons, color in flowers growing in the grass.

Egg Carton Flowers on Pipe Cleaner Stems

☆ **Tools:**
scissors
paint brush

✱ ★ **Materials:**
clay or homemade claydough
  (see page 24)
paper cup
pipe cleaners cut in 3" pieces
3 sections of a cardboard egg
  carton
watercolor paints
container of water for paint
  brush

Directions

1. Cut small triangles into edges of each cardboard egg section to make flower petals.
2. Paint each section (or flower) a different color, and push the end of a pipe cleaner through the center of each one.
3. Put a small ball of clay into the paper cup "flower pot".
4. Push the pipe cleaner stems into the clay base.

Paper Bag Bunny

☆ **Tools:**
scissors
glue
markers or crayons

✱ ★ **Materials:**
small brown paper bag
cotton puff
yarn pieces for whiskers and
  trim

Directions

1. Turn bag upside down with open end towards the bottom.
2. Pull out sides of bag and spread bag flat on the table. (The open end of the bag will be the bottom of the bunny).
3. Draw side view of bunny (circle head, oval body, small circle tail, elongated oval ear, short oval legs),
4. Cut along top and bottom lines with scissors.
5. Do not cut on sides where bag is folded.
6. Reposition the bag along original fold lines when opened, and stand the bunny up.
7. Draw features on the face.
8. Glue on yarn whisker trim and cotton puff tail.

Mother's Day Gift Ideas

☆ **Tools:**
*paint brush—or dishpan filled
  with 2" of water*

 ★ **Materials:**
*several colors tempera paint
paint trays
12" dowel rod
twine or yarn
8" x 10" piece of burlap material
glue
          or
small bottle any color India ink
several sheets white paper (typing paper)
3 or 4 small white envelopes
iron*

Directions

BURLAP WALL HANGING

1. Fray three edges of the piece of burlap by pulling strings.
2. Turn unfrayed (top) edge of burlap under to make a 1" hem.
3. Glue edge (if adult has not machine stitched) to secure.
4. Paint an original, colorful picture with tempera.
5. When dry, insert dowel rod.
6. Tie twine or yarn to ends of dowel rod so burlap may be hung.

STATIONERY

1. Drop three or four drops of India ink into water in dishpan.
2. Blow on the ink spots to swirl in water.
3. Quickly immerse one sheet of white paper into the water and immediately remove.
4. Lay on sheets of newspaper to dry.
5. Stain each sheet of paper and the flap of each envelope in this way.
6. If the water begins to "muddy", pour it out, refill the dishpan with clean water, drop in more ink and continue the process.
7. The ink will dye the paper with swirls of color.
8. When the paper dries, it can be ironed to smooth and flatten.

Cotton Puff Caterpillar

☆ **Tools:**
scissors
glue
crayons

★ **Materials:**
4 cotton puffs
green tissue paper strip, 8" long,
*   3" wide*
small scraps colored construc-
*   tion paper*

Directions

1. Fringe green tissue strip along one side with scissors.
2. Glue to bottom of construction paper.
3. Glue cotton puffs in a row for caterpillar's body. (Nestle the cotton puffs in the fringed, green grass).
4. Cut eyes, antenna, tiny strips for feet, etc. from construction paper scraps and glue into place.
5. Using crayons, draw details: flowers, trees, clouds, birds.

Mother's Day Card

☆ **Tools:**
scissors
glue
crayons or markers

★ **Materials:**
1 sheet white construction paper
red and white tissue squares

Directions

1. Fold white paper in half to form card.
2. On front of card, in upper left hand corner, glue crushed tissue squares to form the shape of a bouquet of flowers.
3. With green crayon, draw long stems and leaves.
4. Write a message on the front of the card.
5. Use crayons to draw a personal, creative picture inside the card.

Bunny in a Coat, page 96

Forsythia Bush

☆ **Tools:**
glue
brown crayon

★ **Materials:**
1 sheet colored construction
  paper
30-40 1" yellow tissue squares
10 2" green tissue squares
short length of yarn or ribbon

Directions

1. With brown crayon draw 5 or 6 stems in the center of the construction paper.
2. Dot glue along stems.
3. Crush yellow tissue and glue each piece over a dot of glue.
4. Twist green tissue into leaf or bow shapes and glue in random pattern along the stems.
5. Tie ribbon or yarn into a big bow, and glue to the bottom of the stems.

Spring Bouquet

☆ **Tools:**
scissors
glue
glue brush

★ **Materials:**
1 sheet green construction paper
1 sheet pastel colored construc-
  tion paper
several sheets of different col-
  ored tissue paper, cut into 4"
  squares
8" piece of ribbon or yarn

Directions

1. Cut leaf shapes (ovals) from green construction paper.
2. Crush each square of tissue into a loose ball.
3. Cover a large area in center of pastel paper with glue and arrange tissue balls into a boquet.
4. Glue leaves around edges of bouquet.
5. Tie ribbon into a bow and glue to bottom of bouquet.

Paper Plate Porcupine

☆ **Tools:**
scissors
glue
brown and black crayons

✳ ★ **Materials:**
1 large paper plate
box of toothpicks

Directions

1. Cut paper plate in half.
2. Cut the center from one of the plate halves.
3. Using this center section, cut two rectangles with rounded edges for the porcupine's feet.
4. Glue the paper plate rim section to the edge of the other paper plate half.
5. Glue the feet shapes to the bottom of the solid plate half.
6. Color the figure with the brown crayon; draw small black eye and whiskers.
7. Dot the figure with glue.
8. Break toothpicks in half and glue one piece to each glue dot.

Stuffed Bag Teddy Bear

☆ **Tools:**
scissors
glue
crayons

✳ ★ **Materials:**
small brown paper bag
1 sheet brown construction
  paper
sheets of newspaper
10" length ribbon

Directions

1. To draw Teddy Bear pieces: head is large circle with small, half-circle ears; arms are flat oval shapes; legs are short rectangles with rounded edges.
2. Draw shapes on brown construction paper and cut with scissors.
3. Detail features, toes, etc. with crayons.
4. Stuff bag with newspaper and twist to close bag.
5. Glue legs to bottom of bag, arms to sides of bag, head at top of bag in front of the twisted closure (bear's neck).
6. Tie ribbon around bear's neck with big bow.

Green Claydough Snake

Alligator with Meat Tray Teeth

☆ **Tools:**
scissors
glue

 ★ **Materials:**
claydough (see recipe, page 124) mixed with green food coloring
cookie decorations ("Silver Decors")
small scrap red felt or red construction paper

Directions
1. Knead dough until workable.
2. Divide into small portions and roll into snake shape.
3. Press cookie decoration eyes into place and secure with a drop of glue.
4. Cut a small forked tongue from red felt or paper and glue into place.
5. Set aside to dry for the rest of the day.

☆ **Tools:**
scissors
glue
black crayon or marker

★ **Materials:**
1 sheet green construction paper
styrofoam meat or vegetable tray
small metal brad

Directions
1. To draw an alligator: large oval body with curving, triangle tail; wedge shaped mouth on opposite end of oval shape; draw rectangles lying parallel to the oval shaped body for front and back feet.
2. Cut along outside lines to cut out the figure—cut a small "bump" on top the alligator's head for the eye.
3. Use crayon or marker to draw small inverted "v" shapes over the alligator's back (scales), and draw eye slit in the center of the "bump" for detail.
4. Draw toes on the feet.
5. Using scissors, completely cut off the lower part of the mouth wedge (jaw).
6. Re-attach with metal brad so jaw will move up and down.
7. Cut two small strips of jagged white teeth from the styrofoam meat tray, and glue to back of alligator's mouth.

Stand-Up Duck

☆ **Tools:**
scissors
glue
pencil

★ **Materials:**
*1 sheet yellow construction
  paper*
*1/2 sheet yellow construction
  paper*
*1/4 sheet orange construction
  paper*
1/4 sheet blue construction paper

Directions

1. Roll larger sheet of yellow paper into a tube, short sides together, and glue to secure.
2. On 1/2 sheet yellow paper draw two wing shapes (ovals or triangles with feathered edges) and jagged-edge triangle for tuft of feathers at top of head.
3. Cut two large circles from blue paper for eyes.
4. Cut bill shape (arrowhead shape with rounded point and tab at bottom for glue flap) from orange paper.
5. Stand yellow tube up on one end.
6. Glue wings to sides of tube near bottom.
7. Glue feather tuft to inside top edge.
8. Glue eyes near top of tube.
9. Attach bill shape by folding under the tab and applying glue.

Paper Helicopter

☆ **Tools:**
scissors
crayons

★ **Materials:**
1 sheet construction paper

Directions

1. Draw a rectangle, 2" wide, along short edge of construction paper.
2. Above the rectangle shape draw a large circle, covering the rest of the paper and slightly overlapping the rectangle shape.
3. Cut along the outside line of the two shapes—do not cut into two pieces—so the resulting shape is a large circle connected to a horizontal rectangle.
4. Starting at the top edge of the circle, draw a vertical line extending to within 1 inch of the opposite edge of the circle.
5. Cut along this line.
6. Bend one of the half-circle flaps down toward the rectangle.
7. Turn the shape over and bend the other half-circle flap down toward the rectangle.
8. Fold 1/3 of the rectangle in toward its center.
9. Fold 1/3 of the rectangle on the other side in toward the center. (You now have a folded square at the bottom of the circle.)
10. Fold the corners of the square in at the bottom to make a point.
11. Throw the shape into the air and it will twirl to the ground.
12. The helicopter can be decorated with crayons.

Boat

☆ **Tools:**

scissors
glue
crayons or markers

★ **Materials:**

1 sheet blue construction paper
1/2 sheet green construction
  paper
1/2 sheet red construction paper
1/2 sheet yellow construction
  paper
1/2 sheet white construction
  paper

Directions

1. Draw a large oval shape on the red construction paper.
2. Draw a line to divide the oval in half.
3. Cut out this half-oval shape. (This is the bottom of the boat.)
4. Trim edges of green paper to make a smaller rectangle shape which will fit over the red oval. (This is the body of the boat.)

5. Cut a smokestack from the yellow paper (square with small rectangle cut from center edge.)
6. Cut large white clouds from white paper.
7. Draw three circles across the middle of the green rectangle body of the boat.
8. Cut out these circles (portholes.)
9. Glue paper pieces to blue backing sheet in this order: white clouds at top of paper; yellow smokestack over clouds; green boat body under smokestack; red oval bottom under green body.
10. Cut away blue paper under portholes.
11. Using scraps, draw figures of people and cut with scissors.
12. Detail features, clothes on the people, waves under the boat, fish in the water, flag on top of boat, etc. with crayons or markers.
13. Insert people into the portholes so that head and shoulders show, and glue into place.

Toilet Tissue Roll Airplane

 ☆ **Tools:**
scissors
glue
crayons

★ **Materials:**
1/2 sheet blue construction paper
small black construction paper
  scrap
cardboard toilet tissue roll
colored stick-on stars

Directions

1. Using scissors, cut slit on each side of cardboard roll to middle of the tube.
2. Fold sheet of blue paper in half and draw a parallelogram with long sides about 3 or 4 inches (short side of parallelogram is folded edge).
3. Cut out this shape with scissors.
4. Do not cut on folded edge.
5. Cut two small circle wheels from black paper scrap.
6. Cut a small rectangle from blue paper scraps, and cut off one corner to make tail section.
7. Fold opposite short edge of rectangle to make a tab.
8. Glue tail section to cardboard roll by applying glue to the tab (make sure to hold cardboard roll so that the slits are on the sides.)
9. Unfold the blue paper and insert the wedge shape (wings) into the slits on the cardboard roll with the point of the wedge as the nose of the plane.
10. Glue on black circle wheels.
11. Use colored stars to decorate on wing tips, tail section, side of plane.

Bus

☆ **Tools:**
scissors
glue
crayons

★ **Materials:**
1 sheet yellow construction paper
old magazines

Directions

1. Fold yellow paper in half, lengthwise.
2. Work with folded edge toward the top.
3. Draw a line along the bottom of the paper, including half-circle wheel shapes, to make the bottom of the bus.
4. Cut along this line with scissors.
5. Draw details on the sides of the bus, including windows, front window, doors, headlights, bumper, lettering, etc.
6. Cut pictures of people (head and shoulders) from magazines and glue into windows of the bus.
7. When unfolded, the bus will stand.

Rigatoni and Cereal Choo-Choo Train

☆ **Tools:**
scissors
glue
paint brush

★ **Materials:**
1 sheet any color construction paper
1/4 sheet black construction paper
small handful of Cheerios®
small handful of rigatoni
container of water for paints
watercolors

Directions

1. Using scissors, cut a rectangle shape for the locomotive.
2. Cut a small rectangle and cut off the corners on one end to make a wedge-shaped smokestack.
3. Glue the locomotive with smokestack over one end at the bottom of the construction paper.
4. To make the cars behind the engine, glue pieces of rigatoni along the bottom of the paper.
5. Glue Cheerios underneath the pasta cars for wheels.
6. Glue Cheerios coming out of the smokestack and drifting across the construction paper at the top in a wavy line to resemble smoke.
7. Using watercolors, paint the rigatoni train cars bright colors.
8. Paint the Cheerio wheels black.
9. Crush a few pieces of rigatoni and glue to black paper locomotive for windows.
10. Paint these pieces yellow.

Postman's Mailbag and Mailbox

☆ **Tools:**
scissors
glue
tape
stapler
paint brush
black marker

★ **Materials:**
1 large brown grocery bag
2 sheets blue construction paper
1 small scrap white construction
  paper
stick-on stars
hair spray or spray starch
red, white and blue tempera
  paint
paint trays

Directions

POSTMAN'S MAILBAG

1. Cut about three inches from the top of the grocery bag.
2. Use this strip for the mailbag strap.
3. Fold cut edge of bag over about 1" to strengthen.
4. Staple strap (paper strip) to each side of the bag.
5. Using tempera, paint mail bag red, white and blue.
6. Spray with hair spray or starch.

MAILBOX

1. Turn one sheet of blue paper so that short sides are at top and bottom.
2. Cut edges off top corner so that mailbox will have a domed top.
3. Cut along bottom edge to make short square legs for the mailbox.
4. Using the other sheet of blue paper, cut off the four corners to make a large oval shape.
5. Turn paper oval so that short sides are at top and bottom.
6. Draw a vertical line to cut off 1/4 of the side of the oval, and cut along this line with scissors. (The oval shape now has one flat side.)
7. Turn the oval flat edge down.
8. Fold in each side of the oval 1/3 so that the resulting shape is a square.
9. Outline this square with black marker and add detail such as a slit for inserting letters, hinges at the bottom, lettering. (This square made from the folded oval is the door to the mailbox shape.)
10. Lay the square on the front of the large blue mailbox shape, and trace the length of the square's sides on the bigger shape.
11. Using scissors, cut slits on the sides of the square (not at top and bottom), and slip folded flaps of the door into the slits so the door can be opened at the top as if the bottom edge were hinged. (On the back of the mailbox, run a length of tape from the bottom edge of one folded flap to the other, so when mailbox door is opened, the edges won't slip out of the slits.)
12. Cut the white paper scrap into a rectangle and glue to the top of the mailbox to represent the mail pick-up schedule.
13. Add details with black marker and stick-on stars.

Fireman's Hat

☆ **Tools:**
scissors
glue
black marker

★ **Materials:**
1 large sheet (12" x 18") red construction paper
1/4 sheet yellow construction paper

Directions

1. Cut edges off corners of red paper to make large oval shape.
2. In center of oval draw a large semi-circle (curving up) with a 7-8" diameter.
3. Cut along this curved line, and fold the flap up.
4. Cut the flap into a pointed, dome shape.
5. The hat fits the child by putting the head into the semi-circle hole.
6. Draw a badge or shield on the scrap of yellow paper and cut with scissors.
7. Detail with marker such as lettering, numbers or name on the shield, and draw a large "V" with a few parallel lines at the front of the hat shape to add dimension.
8. Glue shield to hat.

Doctor's Head-band and Bag

☆ **Tools:**
scissors
glue
crayons

★ **Materials:**
2 sheets black construction
  paper
1 sheet white construction paper
1 small scrap white or red paper
small aluminum foil circle, (2"
  diameter)

Directions
DOCTOR'S HEADBAND
1. Cut two strips, 2 inches wide, from long edge of black construction paper.
2. Glue two ends together; when glue dries, fit around the head and glue remaining two ends together.

3. Glue foil circle to middle of the headband for doctor's light.

DOCTOR'S BAG
1. Fold sheet of black construction paper in half, top to bottom.
2. Glue sides together along the edges of the paper.
3. Cut handles (rectangles folded in half—cut smaller rectangle shape from inside) and glue to each side of the open end of the folded paper.
4. Cut red or white paper cross (two, crossed rectangles) and glue to side of doctor's bag.
5. Use white paper and crayons to draw pictures of doctor's "helpers": Syringe, stethoscope, rubber hammer, thermometer, bottle of medicine, etc.
6. These can be cut out and put into the bag, or the sheet of paper can be folded and slipped inside the bag.

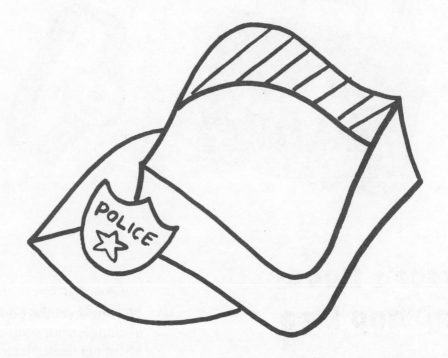

Policeman's Hat

☆ **Tools:**
scissors
glue
tape
crayons or markers

★ **Materials:**
1 sheet blue construction paper
1 small yellow paper scrap

Directions
1. Fold blue paper in half, lengthwise.
2. Cut along fold line to divide paper in half.
3. Fold one half sheet in half, lengthwise.

4. Cut along this fold line to make two strips for the headband.
5. Glue two ends together; when dry, measure around head and glue the other two ends together.
6. Using remaining half sheet construction paper, draw a large moon shape (semi-circle) for the brim of the hat.
7. Glue to the headband at the top edge of the brim.
8. Cut a shield or badge shape from the yellow paper.
9. Detail with a large star, number, lettering, etc.
10. Cut out this shield and glue to center of headband, over the brim.

Crossing Guard with Stop Sign

☆ Tools:
scissors
glue
crayons or markers

★ Materials:
1 sheet blue construction paper
large white, green, red and
*   yellow paper scraps*
1 popsicle stick
1 gold stick-on star

Directions

1. Draw a crossing guard on the blue paper: Circle head; rectangle body; small rectangle legs, oval shoes; long uplifted rectangle-shaped arms, small circle hands.

2. On yellow paper, draw yellow mittens to fit over the crossing guard's hands.

3. Draw a "T" shaped crossing guard belt.

4. Draw a yellow policeman type hat (rectangle with semi-circle brim).

5. Cut out these pieces and glue to the crossing guard figure.

6. Cut out the crossing guard.

7. Detail with crayons or markers.

STOP SIGN

1. Draw a square on each scrap of white, green and red paper scraps. (Draw the red and green squares slightly smaller than the white square.)

2. Cut large sections off each corner to make an eight-sided stop sign.

3. Glue the green piece to one side of the white piece.

4. Lay popsicle stick on the other side of the white piece and glue red piece over this.

5. Write "GO" on the green side; "STOP" on the red side.

Mail Truck

☆ **Tools:**
scissors
glue
black crayon or marker

★ **Materials:**
1 sheet blue construction paper
1/2 sheet red construction paper
1/2 sheet white construction
  paper
scraps of black and yellow con-
  struction paper
small piece of cellophane food
  wrap

Directions

1. Cut corners off one side of the blue paper to make the basic mail truck shape have a slightly domed top.
2. Glue the red paper behind the blue paper so that about 1 inch of the red paper shows at the top edge.
3. Fold the half sheet of white paper in half and cut along folded edge.
4. Cut one corner off the white paper rectangle to make the top of the mail truck shape.
5. Draw a large rectangle window in the white shape and cut out with scissors.
6. Glue cellophane food wrap piece behind the window section.
7. Glue the white paper to the top of the truck, behind the red piece.
8. Cut two large black circles and two small yellow circles from the scrap paper.
9. Glue smaller yellow circles in center of large black circle wheels.
10. Glue wheels to bottom of truck.
11. Cut a star or other decorative shape from the yellow paper scrap and glue to side of truck.
12. Use black crayon or marker to add details: headlight, step, door, bumper, etc.

Musician's Instruments (three examples)

☆ **Tools:**
scissors
glue
markers

★ **Materials:**
1 sheet white construction paper

FOR GUITAR: 1 sheet brown
  construction paper
4 6" lengths of black yarn

FOR HORN: 1/2 sheet black
con   struction paper (cut
lengthwise)
6 or 7 dried beans

FOR DRUM: 1 sheet blue con-
struction paper
4 popsicle sticks
3 tissues 1 torn in half

Directions

GUITAR
1. Cut a 1-2" strip from the short edge of the brown paper.
2. This is the neck of the guitar.
3. Draw an hourglass shape on the remaining piece of brown paper, and cut out this piece with scissors.
4. Also cut a circle in the middle of the shape by folding shape in half and cutting a half circle on the fold.
5. Glue the two pieces to the sheet of white construction paper.
6. Drizzle glue in long lines from top of guitar neck, across the hole and down to bottom of guitar.
7. Lay yarn strings on the glue, pulling them straight.

HORN
1. Draw a horn shape on the black paper: long rectangle shape with one end opening into a triangle and the other end pointed to make the mouthpiece.
2. Cut out this shape and glue to white construction paper.
3. Glue on dried beans to represent the keys.

DRUM
1. Cut a large square from the blue construction paper, and glue to the bottom of the white paper.
2. To make each tympany drum stick, glue two popsicle sticks together, end to end.
3. Crush one tissue and cover smoothly with half of another, tucking ends up under the ball and gluing to white paper at one end of the stick.

NOTE: Details could be added to each of these pictures with markers.

Buds on Branches

☆ **Tools:**
glue

★ **Materials:**
*1 sheet pastel colored construc-
  tion paper
dried pinto beans
several twigs (about 8" long)
alternate material: puffed wheat
  cereal instead of dried beans*

Directions

1. With short edge of construction paper at the bottom, glue twigs to paper.
2. With a drop of glue to hold each, glue a bean every few inches along the twigs to represent buds.

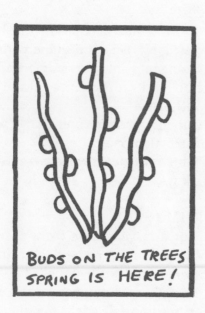

BUDS ON THE TREES
SPRING IS HERE!

Recipes

CLAYDOUGH RECIPE

★ **Materials:**
*2 cups flour
1 cup salt
2 cups water
few tablespoons cooking oil*

1. Mix flour, salt and enough water to make dough.
2. Add a little oil to keep mixture from being too sticky.
3. Make several smaller balls of claydough and knead until workable.

SOAP PAINT RECIPE

★ **Materials:**
*powdered tempera paint
bar of soap
1/2 cup liquid starch
2 cups water*

1. Using a metal grater, grate the bar soap into flakes.
2. Mix the soap flakes with tempera, liquid starch and water.
3. Beat until very thick and creamy.

INDEX

INDEX

INDEX

INDEX